MADAME DE SÉVIGNÉ

MADAME DE SÉVIGNÉ

SOME ASPECTS OF
HER LIFE AND CHARACTER

by

ARTHUR TILLEY

FELLOW OF KING'S COLLEGE
CAMBRIDGE

CAMBRIDGE
AT THE UNIVERSITY PRESS
1936

CAMBRIDGE
UNIVERSITY PRESS

University Printing House, Cambridge CB2 8BS, United Kingdom

Cambridge University Press is part of the University of Cambridge.

It furthers the University's mission by disseminating knowledge in the pursuit of education, learning and research at the highest international levels of excellence.

www.cambridge.org
Information on this title: www.cambridge.org/9781316620045

© Cambridge University Press 1936

First published 1936
First paperback edition 2016

A catalogue record for this publication is available from the British Library

ISBN 978-1-316-62004-5 Paperback

To

MY WIFE

CONTENTS

PREFACE

This is not a life of Mme de Sévigné. It is merely an attempt to bring out in fuller detail than hitherto certain aspects of it. The first chapter calls attention to the accuracy of her information about current events and to the marvellous skill with which she describes an event at which she was not present. The second chapter gives some account of her more intimate friends, and at the same time shews her remarkable capacity for true friendship. The next chapter calls attention to her love of the country as well as of society and to the need which she had from time to time of solitary meditation on serious subjects. It was at her country home of Les Rochers that she did most of her reading, and thus we pass naturally in the last chapter to an examination of the books that she read. She liked good company, as she calls Montaigne, in books as well as in real life. Character in action appealed to her more than the delicate analysis of it. Thus she preferred *Tartuffe* to *Le Misanthrope*, and *Cléopâtre* to *Bérénice* and perhaps even to *La Princesse de Clèves*. For the same reason she delighted in history, especially when it dealt with incident and character. In later life books of religious controversy as well as history attracted her. She had always had her favourite books of devotion.

Besides her letters the chief sources for Mme de Sévigné's life are the biographical notice by P. Mesnard which forms the first volume of the edition by Monmerqué and Mesnard, 14 vols., 1862–1866, in the *Grands Écrivains de la France* and Walckenaer's *Mémoires touchant la vie et les écrits de Mme de Sévigné*, 5 vols., 1842–1852, to which a sixth volume was added by Aubenas in 1865. It cannot be said that either work gives us a satisfactory life. Mesnard's is unattractive in style and badly put together. Walckenaer's discursive volumes supply much information about the society and events of Mme de Sévigné's day, but they often fail us in matters which concern her inner life and character. The two writers who seem to me to have understood her best are Sainte-Beuve (*Portraits de Femmes*) and Gaston Boissier (*Les Grands Écrivains français*, 1887). There are recent studies by André Hallays (1920) and Cécile Gazier (1933), and two English women of genius, Lady Ritchie (Annie Thackeray) and Mme Duclaux (Mary Robinson), have paid graceful and characteristic tributes to her memory, the former in *Foreign Classics for English Readers*, the latter in an introductory essay to *Mme de Sévigné's Letters to her daughter*, 10 vols., 1927. Edward FitzGerald's *Dictionary of Mme de Sévigné*, 2 vols., 1914, is notable as a record of the author's devotion, but it required a more complete revision than the piety of his great-niece, Mary Eleanor FitzGerald Kerritch, has permitted. There is a useful little volume entitled *The Queen of Letter-writers*, 1907, by Janet Aldis, and a good selection of letters edited by Professor Baker, Manchester, 1925.

The text that I have used for the letters is that of the edition in the *Grands Écrivains de la France*, but I have cited them by their date as being more convenient for readers who possess other editions. In 1872 a MS. was discovered at Dijon, which contained, besides several new letters, a good many corrections and new fragments. These were used by Ch. Capmas for his *Lettres inédites à Mme de Grignan*, 2 vols., 1876.

A. T.

CAMBRIDGE
1936

I

MME DE SÉVIGNÉ & THE NEWS

On 4 February 1671, Mme de Sévigné was parted from her daughter for the first time in their lives. It was for her a cruel separation, but we owe to it the correspondence which reveals her as the greatest letter-writer of France, perhaps of the world. For it cannot be too clearly recognised that her letters to Mme de Grignan greatly exceed in importance all the rest. In the first place she could write to her daughter, as she could to hardly anyone else, without the fear of her letters being shewn to the wrong people, and this gives them their greatest charm—their absolute spontaneity. Secondly, seeing that her daughter was never absent from her heart or her thoughts and that in fact her whole existence was bound up in her, she could be her true self, she could lay bare her inmost soul.

She herself fully realises the difference between her letters to her daughter and to others:

Je n'aime point m'enivrer d'écriture. J'aime à vous écrire, je parle à vous, je cause avec vous: il me seroit impossible de m'en passer; mais je ne multiple point ce goût: le reste va, parce qu'il le faut.[1]

and a little later she writes:

Je donne avec plaisir le dessus de tous les paniers, c'est-à-dire, la fleur de mon esprit, de ma tête, de mes yeux, de ma plume, de mon écriture; et puis le reste

[1] 9 October 1675.

va comme il peut. Je me divertis autant à causer avec vous, que je laboure avec les autres.[1]

There is some exaggeration in the last sentence. For she evidently took real pleasure in writing to her two cousins, Coulanges and Bussy-Rabutin, both of whom she had known from childhood.[2] But her letters to them do not reveal the whole woman. Rather they bring out certain aspects of her character, since, like all good letter-writers, she unconsciously adopted a tone that suited the character of her correspondent. With Coulanges, to whom three or four of her most brilliant letters are addressed, she is all gaiety and light-heartedness. To Bussy, with whom she was in strong sympathy, a sympathy rather of the head than of the heart—"Autrefois nous avions le don de nous entendre avant que d'avoir parlé"—she writes in a tone of friendly understanding. But her letters to him sometimes give us the feeling that his reputation as a letter-writer and literary critic puts some constraint upon her freedom, or at any rate keeps her from the grammatical escapades which are so delightful in her letters to her daughter. As the years go on, her letters to Bussy become more serious, and in those of the last ten years of her life there are often passages of grave moral reflection. Even in one of her letters to Coulanges, when he was at Rome in 1691 with the Duc de Chaulnes, she writes in a serious vein, beginning with a reflection on the sudden death of Louvois, and then, after dwelling

[1] 1 December 1675.
[2] We have twenty-seven letters to Coulanges and about one hundred and forty to Bussy.

on the great part that the Popes and the Christian religion had played in the great city, recommending her
cousin to read St Augustine on the *Truth of Religion*
and reminding him that, whatever intrigues went on in
the Conclave, it was always the Holy Spirit who made the
Pope: "Voilà sur quoi je vous laisse, mon cher cousin."[1]

We can parallel this difference between Mme de
Sévigné's letters to her daughter and those that she
wrote to others from our own great letter-writers.
Gray's letters to his old schoolfellow, Tom Wharton,
give us a deeper insight into his character than those
to any other of his friends. Horace Walpole is most
natural when he is writing to George Montagu. We
know Dorothy Osborne's charming personality so well,
because all her letters are addressed to her lover and
future husband, with whom she was in perfect sympathy.

Another reason for Mme de Sévigné's delightful
spontaneity is that she is so little conscious of her
matchless skill: "Est-il possible, ma très-chère," she
writes, when she was past sixty, "que j'écrive bien?
cela va si vite; mais puisque vous êtes contente, je ne
demande pas davantage." And twenty years earlier she
wrote to her cousin, Bussy, "Il seroit à souhaiter que
ma pauvre plume, galoppant comme elle fait, galoppât
au moins sur le bon pied." But she was, as she says,
quite content with the pleasure that her letters gave her
daughter. "Je suis ravie, ma chère bonne," she writes
on her forty-sixth birthday (5 February 1672), "que
vous aimez mes lettres. Je ne crois pas pourtant

[1] 26 July 1691—a remarkable letter.

qu'elles sont aussi agréables que vous dîtes; mais il est vrai que pour figées, elles ne le sont pas." Certainly nothing could be less "congealed" than Mme de Sévigné's letters. They flow from one topic to another like conversation. "Voilà bien de la conversation," she says in another letter, "car c'est ainsi qu'il faut appeler mes lettres; car si celle-ci vous ennuye, j'en suis fâchée, car je l'ai écrite de bon cœur, et *currente calamo*."[1]

This is no mock-modesty, in spite of the fact that Mme de Sévigné knew that her letters were talked about and that her friends passed them on from one to another. For instance Mme de Coulanges writes to her that Mme de Thianges (a sister of Mme de Montespan) has sent a lackey to borrow the "Letter about the horse" and the "Letter about the meadow", and she adds: "Vos lettres font tout le bruit qu'elles méritent, comme vous voyez; il est certain qu'elles sont délicieuses et vous êtes comme vos lettres."[2]

Mme de Sévigné must of course have realised that she had a happy knack—as she would modestly have put it—of describing scenes and occurrences in a graphic and amusing fashion, and that this gave much pleasure to her friends. But it certainly did not occur to her that she was a great writer, much less that after her death her letters would be collected and published,

[1] 3 November 1688.
[2] III, 198. The *Lettre de la Prairie* (II, 291) contains the famous description of how Mme de Sévigné sent all her household at Les Rochers to turn hay. The *Lettre du Cheval* is lost. The account of the fire at M. Guitaut's (II, 72 ff.) was known as the *Lettre de l'Incendie*.

like those of Voltaire, of which new editions were continually appearing. She would have been amazed if she had known that by virtue of these letters, written *de bon cœur et currente calamo*, she would one day be recognised as one of the greatest of French classics, and that as such she would inaugurate alike the *Grands Écrivains Français* and the *Grands Écrivains de la France*.

In contrast with Mme de Sévigné's humble opinion of her own letters is the high praise that she gives to her daughter's. This she does constantly. I will quote one passage as a sample of the rest. It is taken from a letter, which from the variety of its topics and from the light that it throws on Mme de Sévigné's thoughts, reading, and friends is one of the first interest:

Ma bonne, ne me parlez plus de mes lettres. Je viens d'en recevoir une de vous, qui enlève, tout aimable, toute brillante, toute pleine de tendresse: un style juste et court, qui chemine et qui plaît au souverain degré je dis même sans vous aimer comme je fais....Il y a un petit air de dimanche gras répandu sur votre dernière lettre, qui la rend d'un goût nonpareil.[1]

We must allow for the partiality of a fond mother, but, as a matter of fact, the few letters of Mme de Grignan that have come down to us are well written and shew decided ability and intelligence. As for the air of Carnival Sunday and the gaiety that Mme de Sévigné detects in them—"Vous êtes plus gaie dans vos lettres que vous ne l'êtes ailleurs"—one associates it more with the mother than with the daughter.

Two days later Mme de Sévigné tells her daughter

[1] 9 March 1672.

what her practice was with regard to answering her letters.[1] The post from Provence arrived in Paris on Monday and Wednesday, and the post for Provence left on Wednesday and Friday. It took a week either way. On Monday Mme de Sévigné began her answer to her daughter's letter as soon as she got it—*à la chaude*—finished it on Tuesday, and posted it on Wednesday. On Friday morning she began to answer the letter she had received on the previous Wednesday and finished it that evening in time for the post. Thus her Wednesday letter, as she explains, was generally much longer than her Friday letter, which contained the news of only two or at most three days, and was written on the same day as it was posted. The part that she added in the evening generally contained something of interest, for every Friday she dined *en Bavardin*, that is to say, with the Bishop of Le Mans, M. Lavardin de Beaumanoir—he died in July 1671—and his widowed sister-in-law, Mme de Lavardin. Other habitual guests were La Rochefoucauld, Benserade, the poet and writer of ballets, "qui fait la joie de la compagnie", and Mme de Brissac, the half-sister of Saint-Simon, and thirty years his senior.[2] The *bavardage* was doubtless of a high order, but what is to be noted here is that Mme de Lavardin had a passion for learning and retailing the latest news.

Delays in the post, or other reasons, sometimes caused Mme de Sévigné to modify her practice either by posting on Monday instead of waiting till Wednes-

[1] 11 March 1672.
[2] She died in 1684.

day, or by answering and posting on Thursday the letter she had received on Wednesday. On one occasion indeed she took four days to make up her "packet". Thus, on Friday morning (24 April 1671) she begins, as usual, an answer to the Wednesday letter. Then, in the evening, after dining *en Bavardin*, she continues it *au faubourg*, that is to say, at La Rochefoucauld's hôtel at the corner of the Rue de Seine and the Rue des Beaux Arts. The latest news is that Vatel, Condé's *maître d'hôtel*, had killed himself because the fish for the grand dinner to the King at Chantilly had not arrived in time. On Sunday she is able to give details, and we have the brilliantly written account that everybody knows. On Monday she adds a page or two on general topics. Finally, on Tuesday, after dining at Pomponne on the Marne, about eighteen miles from Paris, with her old friends Arnauld d'Andilly—his son, Pomponne, was absent in Sweden as ambassador—and conversing with him for six hours, she finishes her "packet" at Livry[1] to the accompaniment of the nightingales, and posts it at Paris. "Que dites-vous", she asks, "de l'infinité de cette lettre?"[2] We have not Mme de Grignan's answer, but we know what posterity says.

At a time when the *Gazette*, founded by Théophraste Renaudot in 1631, was the only news-sheet in France, dwellers in the provinces were naturally eager to hear the news from Paris. Mme de Sévigné, therefore, was

---

[1] Livry is about ten miles from Pomponne and about the same from Paris.

[2] II, 183–196.

always anxious to send her daughter the latest information, and her friends knowing this did their best to help her. Some of them, indeed, like Mme de Lavardin, as we have seen, and Mme d'Huxelles, were themselves eager collectors of news. Indeed, Mme d'Huxelles made a regular business of it and kept up a large correspondence for the purpose. Equally indefatigable was d'Hacqueville, who often sent his *gazette* direct to Mme de Grignan, and, when he died in 1678, he was succeeded as a *gazetier* by the Abbé Bigorre, who lodged at one time with Mme de Sévigné in the Hôtel de Carnavalet.

Mme de Sévigné was far from taking all she heard on trust. For instance, in one of her early letters to her daughter (17 April 1671) she laughs at d'Hacqueville for his credulity and gives an instance of a false report that he had sent: "Tout cela est faux et ridicule et ne se dit point dans les bons lieux.... Je vous déclare, ma fille, que je ne vous manderai rien que de vrai."[1] And in a later letter she says:

Quand je vous mande des nouvelles, comptez que je les tiens de gens bien informés; mais ils ne veulent jamais être cités pour les moindres bagatelles. Il y en a d'autres dont je ne prends jamais des nouvelles.

She had a reliable source of information in Mme de Coulanges, who not only frequented the Court and saw much society, but who as niece to Le Tellier, the Minister of War, and first cousin to his son and successor Louvois, had special sources of information. Writing to Mme de Sévigné at the end of 1672,[2] when

[1] 17 April 1671.   [2] III, 175.

the war against Holland was going on, she says, that spending her days at M. Le Tellier's she hears the news as soon as the couriers arrive.

I will give two striking examples of Mme de Sévigné's accuracy in reporting the news. Let us first take her account of Turenne's death in her letter of 9 August 1675,[1] the letter which begins: "Parlons un peu de M. de Turenne." If we compare it with that given by Saint-Hilaire,[2] who was an eyewitness of the catastrophe and whose father's arm was carried off by the same cannon-ball which killed Turenne, we find that there is no essential difference between the two accounts. That of Mme de Sévigné came from a gentleman in Turenne's service.

The second example is equally striking, for Lord Macaulay, who was very careful about the sources of his information, quotes her as if she were an eyewitness, bracketing her with Dangeau, who was almost certainly one, for he was always at the Court, and who kept a matter-of-fact diary, which is extremely reliable. The event for which Macaulay cites them was the reception of James II by Louis XIV at Saint-Germain. This is Mme de Sévigné's account, written on 10 January 1689:

Le lendemain il fut question de l'arrivée du Roi d'Angleterre à Saint-Germain, où le Roi l'attendoit: il arriva tard: Sa Majesté alla au bout de la salle des gardes au devant de lui: le Roi d'Angleterre se baissa fort comme s'il eût voulu embrasser ses genoux: le Roi

---

[1] This letter has the fullest account. See also those of 31 July and 2 August.

[2] *Mémoires*, ed. L. Lecestre, 6 vols. (in progress), 1903–1916.

l'empêcha, et l'embrassa à trois ou quatre reprises, fort cordialement.

Macaulay's version is that James "bowed so low that it seemed as if he was about to embrace his protector's knees. Lewis raised him, and embraced him with brotherly tenderness."[1] This, it will be noticed, is, at any rate as regards the first sentence, almost a literal translation of Mme de Sévigné. She agrees in the main with Dangeau, but the picturesque touch that James seemed as if he was about to embrace Louis's knees is an addition to his dry statement of fact.[2] Again, the exquisitely phrased remarks which Louis made to James, when, on his departure for Ireland, he came to Versailles to say farewell, are translated by Macaulay[3] with some slight amplifications from Mme de Sévigné, who gives them as follows:

Monsieur, je vous vois partir avec douleur: cependant je souhaite de ne vous revoir jamais: mais si vous revenez, soyez persuadé que vous me retrouverez tel que vous me laissez.[4]

As Mme de Sévigné says, "Peut-on dire mieux." Her brief account of James's departure from Whitehall, for which her authority was her friend, the Abbé Bigorre's *Gazette*, is, except for the spelling, fairly correct. The King of England, she writes on 3 January

---

[1] *Works*, II, 347.
[2] "Le roi d'Angleterre se baissa jusqu'à ses genoux." *Mémoires*, II, 292.
[3] *Works*, II, 528.
[4] 2 March 1689. The words "Je vous void partir avec douleur" are not in Dangeau's account (*Mémoires*, II, 339).

1689, "est dans Vittal: je ne sais point écrire ce mot.... Le Prince d'Orange à Saint-Jean, qui est de l'autre côté du jardin." As a matter of fact James left Whitehall on the morning of 28 December 1688, and William did not arrive at St James's till that evening. Naturally Mme de Sévigné was a strong partisan of James's and regarded the Prince of Orange as a usurper. She had heard that he was a second Attila and that Mary was a Tullia, "who would drive bravely over her father's body".

With these credentials Mme de Sévigné's narrative of the decline and fall of Mme de Montespan and the rise of Mme de Maintenon, as it gradually unfolds itself in her letters, may be accepted with confidence. Indeed, it is remarkable, considering the amount of tittle-tattle that must have passed on the subject, how closely she keeps to the truth. It will be seen that only on two occasions her knowledge was at first-hand, once when she was present at the usual after-dinner gathering of the Court, and once when she paid a visit to Mme de Montespan in her bedroom. But she had many friends and acquaintances who went regularly to Court, especially, as we have seen, Mme de Coulanges, who also had the advantage of having kept up her old friendship, which Mme de Sévigné, as we shall see, had once shared, with Mme de Maintenon.

She appears as Mme Scarron for the first time in Mme de Sévigné's correspondence in a letter written on Christmas Day 1671. Mme Scarron, says Mme de Sévigné, had been having supper with them, that is to say at the house of M. de Coulanges, where Mme de

Sévigné was staying.[1] Six days later Mme Scarron again came to supper and with her the Duc de Richelieu, Guilleragues, and the Abbé Têtu, the two latter being both *habitués* of the two allied salons of the Duchesse de Richelieu and Mme d'Albret. It was almost certainly at one of these that Mme de Sévigné and Mme de Coulanges had met her. Other *habitués*, all of whom we meet with in Mme de Sévigné's pages, were M. de Barillon, Mlle d'Aumale, who became the second wife of the Maréchal de Schomberg, and Mlle de Pons, afterwards Mme d'Heudicourt. Three years before this Mme Scarron had consented to become governess to Mme de Montespan's children, and for each of the first two children, the second being the Duc du Maine (born 31 March 1672), she had taken a separate house on the outskirts of Paris.

On 13 January 1672 Mme de Sévigné writes, "Nous soupons tous les soirs avec Mme Scarron: elle a l'esprit aimable et merveilleusement droit"; on 26 February "Mme Scarron, qui soupe ici (she was still staying with M. de Coulanges) tous les soirs, et dont la compagnie est délicieuse, s'amuse et se joue avec votre fille"; and on 16 March, "Mme Scarron vous aime; elle passe ici la carême, et céans presque tous les soirs." When a third child was born[2] (20 June 1672) Mme Scarron gave up the two small houses and moved into a large one at the far end of the Faubourg Saint-Germain, near the barriers and Vaugirard. Mme de Sévigné describes it as a fine house, with a large garden, and large and

---

[1] II, 449 and Capmas, I, 263.
[2] A son who died in 1683; the first child, a daughter, died in 1672.

handsome rooms.[1] It was probably at this time that Mme Scarron carried out her intention of retiring from society and devoting herself to the education of Mme de Montespan's children, an intention which Mme de Sévigné had mentioned in a letter of 31 December 1671: "Mme Scarron sera encore à Paris deux ou trois jours, et puis, adieu pour des siècles." On 26 December 1672 Mme de Coulanges writes to Mme de Sévigné that no living mortal without exception had any intercourse with Mme Scarron. But on 1 December 1673 Mme de Sévigné writes, " J'ai soupé avec l'amie de *Quanto* (Mme de Montespan)", and three days later, "Nous soupâmes encore hier avec Madame Scarron et l'Abbé Têtu chez Mme de Coulanges", and she adds that at midnight they conducted Mme Scarron back to her house. The reason for her having emerged from her solitude was that, Louis XIV having legitimised his bastards, there was no longer any need for secrecy, and she was on the point of moving with her charges to Mme de Montespan's apartments at Versailles. So long as the haughty mistress reigned supreme, Mme de Maintenon, as she became in January 1675, had a more or less peaceful time disturbed only by the vagaries of the favourite's capricious temper. But when Mme de Montespan began to decline in favour, she entered on evil days. The decline began just before Easter 1675, when, as the combined result of Bossuet's exhortations to the King and Mme de Maintenon's to the mistress, the pair agreed to a separation. It is true that it did not last, and that when Louis returned, as his custom was, from

[1] 4 December 1673.

13

the war in July, they came together again. But there
was a marked change. Mme de Montespan hold on
her lover, partly owing to her growing imperiousness
and irritability, was perceptibly weakening. She had
never forgiven Mme de Maintenon for her share in
bringing about the temporary separation, and for the
next four and a half years she made her life almost
intolerable. They are "as antipathetic to one another",
says Mme de Sévigné in a letter of 5 August 1675, "as
black to white". The influence first of one and then
of the other, predominated; it was a struggle between
the King's good and bad angel. And the rivalry was
complicated by affairs with other mistresses, whom
Mme de Sévigné appropriately designates as *mouches*.

On 25 July 1676 she paid one of her rare visits to
Versailles, and she made one of the party that assembled
daily from three to six in "le bel apartement du Roi".
The centre of attraction was the card-table at which the
King, with Mme de Montespan holding his cards, the
Queen, Monsieur Dangeau, and Langlée were playing
reversi. This was a game of pure chance, requiring
neither skill nor judgment, and was thus well suited to
the players, who were among the greatest gamblers in
the kingdom. Mme de Montespan lost 700,000 crowns
one Christmas Day, and the Queen's debts for *bassette*
at her death amounted to 100,000 crowns. Both Langlée
("un homme de rien") and Dangeau owed their great
influence at Court largely to their success in gambling,
coupled with good-temper and perfect probity. Mme
de Sévigné watched Dangeau with great interest. While
the others chattered continually, even disclosing what

they had in their hands, he was never distracted, but took note of their remarks and drew his conclusions. The natural result was that he won, and the others lost. Presently he asked Mme de Sévigné to share his hand. So she joined the royal circle and made her obeisance to the King, "ainsi que vous me l'avez appris", and the King acknowledged it "as if I had been young and beautiful". The Queen asked after her health and Mme de Montespan compared notes with her on the comparative merits of Bourbon and Vichy. She praises the mistress's "surprising beauty"—"she is not half so stout as she was"—and describes her dress in detail. At six o'clock the party broke up and all went out driving, the King with Mme de Montespan, and M. and Mme de Thianges—Mme de Montespan's sister[1]—the Queen in another carriage with the Princesses. Some went in gondolas on the canal, and some listened to music. At ten o'clock they returned to the palace, and a play was performed till midnight, when there was supper (*media noche*).[2]

A fortnight later (7 August 1676) Mme de Sévigné writes that she has just seen some people who have returned from the Court. "They are persuaded that the sovereignty of *Quanto*[3] has never been so firmly established."

[1] Saint-Simon, who saw her when he was a boy, has left a wonderful portrait of Mme de Thianges. He says, "Elle fut de toutes les parties et tous les voyages tant qu'elle le voulut bien" (*Mémoires*, v, 376–378). For a good story about her see Mme de Sévigné, *Lettres*, III, 347.

[2] 29 July 1676.

[3] For an explanation of this name, shortened from *Quantova*, see *Lettres inédites*, II, 159.

Elle se sent au dessus de toutes choses, et ne craint non plus ses petites morveuses de nièces,[1] que si elles étaient charbonnées. Comme elle a bien de l'esprit, elle paroit entièrement délivrée de la crainte d'enfermer le loup dans la bergerie; sa beauté est extrême, et sa parure est comme sa beauté, et sa gaieté comme sa parure.

Thus outwardly Vashti was still triumphant in her insolent beauty. But on 11 September Mme de Sévigné reports as follows:

Tout le monde croit que l'étoile de Mme de Montespan pâlit. Il y a des larmes, des chagrins naturels, des gaietés affectées, des bouderies; enfin, ma bonne, tout finit.

And on 30 September she writes that there is talk of another lady:

Il est certain qu'il y a eu des regards, des façons pour la *bonne femme*...elle est *une autre* et c'est beaucoup... elle ouvriroit le chemin de l'infidélité, et ne serviroit que comme d'un passage à d'autres, plus jeunes et plus ragoûtantes. Voilà nos réflexions.

The *bonne femme* is Mme de Soubise, whose relations with the King were something of a mystery. As her sole object was to get as much as she could out of him for herself and her family, whether rank or honours or jewels or hard cash, she did not care whether she was mistress or friend; and as she had wit as well as beauty she had no difficulty in making herself acceptable

---

[1] The two daughters of Mme de Thianges, the Duchesse de Nevers, and the future Duchesse de Sforza. *Morveuse* is a contemptuous expression to denote extreme youth. Molière uses it in this sense.

to Louis in either capacity.[1] There was no mystery about Mme de Ludres, Canoness of Poussay, who was maid-of-honour, first to the Queen and then to Madame. According to the latter her reign lasted only two years, so that as she was dismissed, with considerable harshness, in 1677, her reign must have begun in the summer of 1675. Mme de Sévigné, in allusion to Quinault's and Lulli's opera of *Isis*, calls her sometimes Io and sometimes Isis, while Mme de Montespan was wont to speak of her as *ce haillon*. After her dismissal the latter seemed to be re-established in favour, and in September 1677 Mme de Sévigné sends her daughter a striking picture of her insolent and triumphant pride:

Ah ! ma fille, quel triomphe à Versailles ! quel orgueil redoublé ! quel solide établissement ! quelle duchesse de Valentinois ![2] quel ragôut même par les distractions et par l'absence ! quelle reprise de possession ! Je fus une heure dans cette chambre: elle étoit au lit, parée, coiffée; elle se reposait pour le *media noche*. . . .Répresentez-vous tout ce qu'un orgueil peu généreux peut faire dire dans le triomphe, et vous en approcherez. On dit que la petite[3] reprendra son train ordinaire chez Madame.[4]

But two years later *Quanto* had another young and beautiful rival in Mlle de Fontanges, "une belle idiote", who had at least the excuse of being in love with the

---

[1] See Saint-Simon, *Mémoires*, II, 79–88. She was the wife of the Duc de Rohan-Soubise, the head of one of the two chief branches of the great Rohan family. He rarely came to Court and professed complete ignorance of his wife's relations with the King.

[2] This, it will be remembered, was Diane de Poitiers's title.

[3] Mme de Ludres.   [4] 11 June 1677.

King. At the same time Mme de Maintenon's influence was rapidly increasing. "*Quanto* et *l'enrhumée* (a name which Mme de Grignan had given her) sont très mal. Cette dernière est toujours parfaitement bien avec le centre des choses, et c'est que fait la rage", reports Mme de Sévigné on 24 November 1679. In the following January Mme de Maintenon was appointed bedchamber-woman to the Dauphine, which gave her an official post at Court and made her independent of Mme de Montespan.

In a letter of 5 January 1680 Mme de Sévigné says that "Mme de Maintenon is the soul of the Court", and in one of 20 March that "she daily increases in favour".[1] In both letters she also refers to Mlle de Fontanges, without mentioning her name. In the first she says:

Pour la personne qu'on ne voit point, et dont on ne parle point, elle se porte parfaitement bien; elle paroît quelquefois, comme une divinité; elle n'a nulle commerce; elle a donné des étrennes magnifiques à la devancière [Mme de Montespan] et à tous les enfants.

and in the second: "*Le char gris* est d'une beauté étonnante."

In an intermediate letter (28 February) she recounts that when the King went with all the Court to meet the Dauphine as a bride there was seen in the court of Saint-Germain a splendid new coach with eight horses "...and inside the coach was the most beautiful person of the Court alone with des Adrets" (one of Madame's maids-of-honour).

[1] The words evidently refer to Mme de Maintenon and not to the Queen. See Capmas, I, 181 f.

Next we hear, evidently through Mme de Coulanges, who had just come from Court, that Mlle de Fontanges is a duchess with a pension of 20,000 crowns, and that she is going to spend Easter at the Abbey of Chelles, which the King had given to her sister, and then Mme de Sévigné goes on:

Voici une manière de séparation qui fera bien de l'honneur à la sévérite du confesseur. Il y a des gens qui disent que cet établissement sent le congé; en vérité je n'en crois rien: le temps nous l'apprendra. Voilà ce qui est present: Mme de Montespan est enragée; elle pleura beaucoup hier; vous pouvez jugez du martyre que souffre son orgueil; il est encore plus outragé par la haute faveur de Mme de Maintenon.[1]

Mme de Sévigné was wrong. Mlle de Fontanges received her final *congé* a month later. She retired with broken health and died a year later. But there was no return to favour for Mme de Montespan. On 18 September Mme de Sévigné reports that Mme de Maintenon spends every evening from six to ten with His Majesty and that the courtiers call her Mme de *Maintenant*. Soon Mme de Montespan was finally dismissed. There were no more mistresses and Louis returned to his Queen. The drama was ended; there only remained the epilogue—the death of the Queen (July 1683) and the King's marriage to Mme de Maintenon (January 1684). There are no letters from Mme de Sévigné to her daughter between November 1680 and September 1684, but on 27 September 1684 she writes: "La place de Mme de Maintenon est unique dans le monde; il n'y en a jamais eu, et il n'y en aura jamais."

[1] 6 April 1680.

19   2-2

The picture of Versailles and the Court, and of the King and his mistresses, that we get from the letters is all the more impressive from the straightforward simplicity of Mme de Sévigné's narrative, and the comparative absence of comment. Although she had to trust largely to the reports of others, she was careful in her choice of informants, and she passes on their reports just as she hears them, without adding any embroidery of her own. On one or two occasions she corrects the information that she has given in a previous letter. She does not moralise, she is not even mildly satirical; she only reports what she hears. Yet underlying what Faguet calls her "smiling resignation to evil" one can detect a note of irony and of a quiet contempt for the King and his mistresses. For the letters cover the last three or four years of Mme de Montespan's reign, when her position was being endangered by "others, younger and more appetising".

Mme de Sévigné had evidently no liking either for Mme de Montespan or her rivals. She pays unstinted admiration to their beauty, but she is fully aware of their greed and self-seeking, and she gives them all, as we have seen, irreverent nicknames. She knew Mme de Ludres fairly well. In one of her early letters (13 March 1671) she tells an amusing story of how Mme de Ludres was bitten by a dog that was supposed to be mad and how, as a cure, she went to Dieppe to throw herself three times into the sea:

Ne trouvez-vous point que Ludres ressemble à Andromède, et Tréville sur un cheval ailé qui tue le monstre.

"Ah, Zesu! Matame de Grignan l'étranze sose t'être zettée toute nue tans la mer."

Mme de Ludres was a native of Alsace, and Mme de Sévigné is fond of imitating her accent. She was on visiting terms with Mme de Soubise:

Je l'ai vue, et lui ai rendu une visite, qu'elle me fit à mon retour de Bretagne. Je l'ai trouvée fort belle, à une dent près qui lui fait un étrange effet au devant de la bouche; son mari est en parfaite santé et fort gai.[1]

And a few days later:

Mme de Soubise a paru avec son mari, deux coiffes, et une dent de moins, à la Cour.

The letter of 27 September 1684 referred to above, in which Mme de Sévigné speaks of Mme de Maintenon's unique position, was written from Les Rochers, where, leaving her daughter at Paris, she had gone to look after her affairs, and where in order to economise she remained, with a few short intervals, for nearly a year. Except for a visit to Bourbon in the late autumn of 1687 she was at Paris with Mme de Grignan from the beginning of September 1685 to the beginning of October 1688. During these last four years, ever since the Truce of Ratisbon (August 1684), "France was in a state of perfect tranquillity". These are the words with which Mme de La Fayette begins her *Memoirs*, and she goes on to tell how the soldiers, released from war, were employed on making an aqueduct in the valley of Maintenon "in order to make the fountains of Versailles play continuously" and so "advance by some

[1] 16 October 1676.

years the King's pleasures". Owing to an outbreak of malaria the mortality was enormous and the work was abruptly ended by the advent of a fresh war. In the last days of September 1688 Louis XIV, in his insatiable love of aggrandisement, attacked Philippsburg, on the right bank of the Rhine. There was no declaration of war; he merely issued a manifesto explaining that it was a measure of defence. As the young Marquis de Grignan, not yet seventeen, was serving as a volunteer in the army that was besieging Philippsburg, it was here that the hopes and anxieties of both Mme de Sévigné and her daughter centred. Mme de Sévigné's friend, Mme d'Huxelles, also had a son there, in high command as a lieutenant-general, while a son of Mme de La Fayette was, like the young M. de Grignan, serving as a volunteer. The defence of the town was stubborn and the siege, conducted by Vauban according to his usual leisurely and scientific methods, proceeded slowly.

It was not till 2 November that Mme de Sévigné, writing at 9 o'clock in the evening, could begin her letter with "Philisbourg est pris, votre fils se porte bien." The news had come from the highest and most authentic source, for Louvois received it while Père Gaillard was preaching before the King on All Saints' Day. On a signal from His Majesty the preacher stopped, and the King announced the news and fell on his knees to thank God. Then Père Gaillard continued his sermon to the admiration of the King and the Court and received a thousand compliments. All this is told by Mme de Sévigné in a letter written the day after her first announcement and was no doubt posted with it.

I wonder if Lord Macaulay supposed that Mme de Sévigné was present on the two occasions when Louis XIV received James II. If so, he is hardly to blame. For Mme de Sévigné possessed in a quite remarkable degree the gift of describing in detail an incident which she had not seen. One of the best examples of this gift is her famous account of the investiture of the new recipients of the order of Saint-Esprit on New Year's Day, 1689—of how M. de Montchevreuil and M. de Villars got hopelessly entangled with one another and how the good M. d'Hocquincourt was in such discomfort from his breeches and stockings that the Dauphin could not help laughing aloud and even the King's majesty was almost discomposed. Yet she was not at Versailles and only heard about the incident from Coulanges. But, brilliant as this description is, it is surpassed by that of Mlle de Louvois's marriage with a grandson of La Rochefoucauld, at which she was present. In a single sentence, in which every word tells, she represents the whole scene to the life:

Magnificence, illustration, toute la France, habits rabattus et rebrochés d'or, pierreries, brasiers de feu et de fleurs, embarras de carrosses, cris dans la rue, flambeaux allumés, reculements et gens roués; enfin le tourbillon, la dissipation, les demandes sans réponses, les compliments sans savoir ce que l'on dit, les civilités sans savoir à qui l'on parle, les pieds entortillés dans les queues: du milieu de tout cela il sortit quelques questions de votre santé, où ne m'étant pas pressée de répondre, ceux qui les faisoient sont demeurés dans l'ignorance et dans l'indifférence de ce qui en est: *ô vanité des vanités !*[1]

"All Mme de Sévigné is in these lines", says Faguet, who rightly quotes them as a first-rate example of "her style; her rapidity, her impetuosity of movement, her use of sparkling and vivacious images, her delicate and barely perceptible malice, her familiar gesture of smiling resignation to the evil side of things, her air of gaiety, her gentle and amiable grace". This is very true, except for the first remark. Mme de Sévigné is not all here. Besides her gaiety and her grace and her smiling resignation to evil she had a serious and reflective vein, which not unfrequently comes to the surface in her letters, especially in those written during the last five or six years of her life. It is instructive to contrast this account of a scene of which she was an eyewitness with that of the investiture at Versailles. Both are equally brilliant, but the second passage reveals the observer at first hand, an observer with ears as well as eyes; above all, an observer quick to detect the underlying significance of smiles and glances and whispers.

But before I leave this subject I will refer to another of her first-hand accounts, an account which is very well known, but which has sometimes, I think, been misinterpreted, and which is a good example of how in a few simple words she can portray an incident in such a way as to give us an insight into the character of the two persons concerned in it. It is part of an

[1] 29 November 1679.

account of how she went to Saint-Cyr to witness a performance of *Esther*, and this is the passage in question:

Le Roi vint vers nos places, et après avoir tourné, il s'adressa à moi, et me dit: "Madame, je suis assuré que vous avez été contente." Moi, sans m'étonner, je réponds: "Sire, je suis charmé; ce que je sens est au dessus des paroles." Le Roi me dit: "Racine a bien de l'esprit." Je lui dis: "Sire, il en a beaucoup; mais en vérité ces jeunes personnes en ont beaucoup aussi: elles entrent dans le sujet, comme si elles n'avoient fait autre chose." Il me dit: "Ah! pour cela, il est vrai." Et puis Sa Majesté m'en alla, et me laissa l'objet de l'envie.[1]

In the evening Mme de Sévigné recounted her *petites prospérités* to the Chevalier de Grignan: " Je suis assurée qu'il ne m'a point trouvé, dans la suite, ni une sotte vanité, ni un transport de bourgeoise." This is quite true. There is neither vanity nor elation in her narrative, merely a natural pleasure at being spoken to by His Majesty, even though it was only twenty-two words. Incidentally it illustrates that lack of conversation which, according to Mme de Maintenon, distinguished Louis XIV.

Mme de Sévigné was too much a child of her age not to share in the general admiration of the French people for their great monarch. On 27 January 1672 she writes to her daughter that she hears with approval and pleasure that she has drunk joyously to the health of the King her master, and she adds: "En vérité, on ne saurait trop louer le Roi; il est encore perfectionné depuis un an." This was written, it may be noted, just

[1] 21 February 1689.

before Louis began the most unjustifiable of all his wars, the war with Holland. But it would not have occurred to Mme de Sévigné or to any of her friends to question the justice of his acts. Ten years later, when the Peace of Nymegen and the subsequent annexation of Strasbourg and other towns had raised France to the zenith of her power, she writes in the same tone to her friend, the President de Moulceau: "Célébrons toujours son grand nom *sur la terre et sur l'onde* et l'admirons dans toutes les occasions."[1]

At other times too she expresses the sentiments of a loyal and admiring subject. But though she admired Louis as a great king who had raised France to pre-eminence among the nations of Europe, she never speaks of him with any particular regard or affection. As we have seen, during the seven years which preceded her letter to the President de Moulceau the scandal of his love-affairs was at its height, and it is almost inevitable that the very marked dislike which Mme de Sévigné had for the royal mistresses should not have been accompanied by some contempt for their lover. There was more outward decorum at Versailles than at Whitehall, but the organised infidelities of Louis were hardly more dignified than the careless promiscuity of his cousin Charles.

[1] 17 April 1682.

II

MME DE SÉVIGNÉ & HER FRIENDS

Mme de Sévigné had a high standard of friendship. Within the large circle of her acquaintances who welcomed her society and admired her lively wit, her gaiety, and her good-humour, there was a chosen band of intimate friends, who appreciated her deeper and more serious qualities, and who had for her the same loyal devotion that she had for them. "Adieu, ma très-chère et très-loyale; j'aime fort ce mot" is the ending of one of her letters to her daughter. It was loyalty of a special kind that prompted and sustained her affection for her relations, even under adverse circumstances. We have a good example of this in her attitude towards Bussy-Rabutin. We all know how abominably he treated her in his libellous *Histoire amoureuse des Gaules*, but yet she forgave him in the end. After seven years silence she wrote him one or two friendly letters, but when he attempted to justify himself, she said firmly that she would forgive him only on condition that he frankly confessed his sins and asked for her pardon.[1] Then he surrendered:

Je vous ai demandé la vie, vous me voulez tuer à terre, cela est un peu inhumain....Cessez donc, petite brutale, de vouloir souffleter un homme, qui se jette à vos pieds, qui vous avoue sa faute, et qui vous prie de le pardonner.[2]

[1] 26 July 1668.   [2] 31 August 1668.

Mme de Sévigné's answer is well known, but it bears repetition:

Levez-vous, Comte: je ne veux point vous tuer à terre; ou reprenez votre épée pour recommencer notre combat. Mais il vaut mieux que je vous donne la vie, et que nous vivions en paix. Vous avouerez seulement la chose comme elle s'est passée, c'est tout ce que je veux. Voilà un procédé assez honnête: vous ne me pouvez plus appeller justement une petite brutale.[1]

Bussy's answer never reached Mme de Sévigné, and two months later she wrote to him again to announce the engagement of "la plus jolie fille de France", as he called Mlle de Sévigné, to the Comte de Grignan. But in spite of this reconciliation the course of friendship did not for some time run smoothly. Bussy was arrogant, vain, and prone to take offence, while Mme de Sévigné, though on the whole she treated him with great tact, could not refrain altogether from little reminders of his past conduct. However, peace was restored at last, and for the remaining thirty-five years of her life Mme de Sévigné's friendship with him was on a far more satisfactory and durable footing than it had ever been. She was no doubt attracted to him by a common interest in literature and a certain similarity of tastes, and also by his reputation as a connoisseur and his talent as a letter-writer.

In one of her letters to him (written in August 1675), she says that she "passes her day with five or six friends (*amies*) in whose society she delights". This gives us a serviceable starting-point. Who were the

[1] 4 September 1668.

five or six friends? Beyond all question the first place belongs to Mme de La Fayette. Many were the hours that she spent in her society, either at Rochefoucauld's *hôtel*, known as the Hôtel de Liancourt, in the Rue de la Seine (on the site of the present Rue des Beaux Arts), or at her own house, with its charming garden, in the Rue de Vaugirard, opposite the Petit-Luxembourg. "I have spent the whole evening with d'Hacqueville in Mme de La Fayette's garden", she writes in July 1674; "there is a fountain and a little shelter; it is the prettiest place in Paris for getting a breath of air." It would be an idle task to attempt to add anything to what has already been so well said about Mme de La Fayette. But I will give two quotations which express to perfection in a few words what these two great women were to one another. One is from a letter that Mme de La Fayette wrote to her friend sixteen days before death came to release her from her constant sufferings. The letter, which is only of a few lines, ends with, "Croyez, ma très-chère, que vous êtes la personne du monde que j'ai le plus véritablement aimée." The other is from a letter written by Mme de Sévigné to Mme de Guitant eight days after Mme de La Fayette's death:

Jamais nous n'avions eu le moindre nuage dans notre amitié.…Ainsi, madame, elle a eu raison après sa mort, et jamais elle n'a été sans cette divine raison, qui était sa qualité principale.[1]

There is no more beautiful page in the history of literature than the friendship between these two women.

[1] 3 June 1693 (x, 107 ff.).

Nor can there be a greater tribute than this friendship to their intrinsic worth, for their standard of friendship was equally high. La Rochefoucauld called Mme de La Fayette *la vraie*, and we have seen what Mme de Sévigné's standard was.

From Mme de La Fayette we naturally pass to La Rochefoucauld, and whatever may have been his faults in the days when he was drawn by vanity into love and by love into political intrigue, and however bitter and disillusioned regrets for his past follies may have made him, there can be no doubt that he was a most delightful and attractive figure in society and a staunch and serviceable friend. In his admirable portrait of him, Cardinal de Retz, while he rightly points out his incapacity for successful intrigue, pays a tribute to his good sense, his gentleness, and his *facilité de mœurs* and he winds up by saying "that he had much better have been contented to pass, as he might have done, for the most polished courtier and the most perfect gentleman (*le plus honnête homme*) in all matters of social life that had appeared in his time". La Rochefoucauld would have been pleased with this last remark, for in his portrait of himself he speaks of his strong desire to be "tout-à-fait honnête homme", while none of his *Maximes* are better or more penetrating than those which he devotes to society and to the qualities of an "honnête homme". His conception of these qualities was a high one, involving as it did, a Christian-like regard for one's neighbour. It follows that an "honnête homme" must almost necessarily be a friend. "J'aime mes amis", he says, "et je les aime d'une façon que je ne balancerais

pas un moment à sacrifier mes intérêts aux leurs", and
in a remarkable maxim he points out in some detail the
duties of true friendship:

On doit aller au-devant de ce que peut plaire à ses
amis, chercher les moyens de leur être utile, leur
épargner les chagrins, leur faire voir qu'on les partage
avec eux quand on ne peut les détourner, les effacer
insensiblement sans prétendre les arracher tout d'un
coup, et mettre en place les objets agréables, ou du
moins qui les occupent.

He himself was such a friend. "Je n'ai jamais vu homme
si obligeant ni si aimable", says Mme de Sévigné. And
when his death left Mme de La Fayette inconsolable
she writes:

Où retrouvera-t-elle un tel ami, une telle société,
une pareille douceur, un agrément, une confiance, une
considération pour elle et pour son fils.

And in a letter to M. de Guitaut she speaks of their
friendship as "un commerce rempli de toute l'amitié
et de toute la confiance possible entre deux personnes
dont le mérite n'est pas commun".[1] A great many of
La Rochefoucauld's maxims deal with love, a subject
on which he believed that he had had some experience.
But, Mme de Sévigné says of him, "Je ne crois pas
que ce s'appelle amoureux il a jamais été."

Hardly less important in Mme de Sévigné's life were
M. and Mme de Coulanges. Their *hôtel* in the Rue du
Parc-Royal was always at her disposal, when, for some
reason or other, her own house was not available. She
stayed there, for instance, over a week, while she was

[1] VII, 344.

moving into the Hôtel de Carnavalet.[1] And when Mme
de Coulanges was dangerously ill in the autumn of
1676, she practically took up her abode there for several
days.[2] Philippe-Emmanuel, Marquis de Coulanges, was
her first cousin. He was seven years her junior, and
she had literally known him all his life. "Le moyen que
vous ne m'aimiez pas? C'est la première chose que
vous avez faite, quand vous avez commencé d'ouvrir
les yeux." They played together in the park at Livry,
and when he married the daughter of M. du Gué-
Bagnols, Intendant of Lyons, she soon became intimate with his wife. The friendship with both remained
unbroken to her death, for they both survived her.
She must have received her last letter from Mme de
Coulanges less than a week before her death. The last
letter of hers that has been preserved was written to
M. de Coulanges. It is a thousand pities that more
of their letters have not survived, for both husband
and wife were excellent letter-writers, and when Mme
de Sévigné was in Brittany or Provence they were
her constant correspondents. Moreover, though they
were perfectly good friends, they went very much
their own ways, and therefore Mme de Sévigné had
in them two separate sources of information. The
letters of both are characteristic. There is more humour
in the husband's, and his information is more con-
secutive and on the whole fuller. Those of the wife,
especially the few that we have of her younger days,
seem to justify the nicknames of *la feuille, la mouche,*

[1] 15, 20 and 22 October 1677.
[2] 25 and 30 September 1676.

and *la sylphide* that Mme de Sévigné gave to her. They shew wit and fantasy, and are pointed by happy expressions, while the bad writing and spelling—these defects we learn from the husband—together with the want of order in the composition, are what one might expect from a charming woman who was somewhat of a scatter-brain. M. de Coulanges seems to have had a stimulating effect on Mme de Sévigné, for it is to him that the famous letters about Mademoiselle's intended marriage to Lauzun[1] and the equally famous *La Prairie*[2] are addressed.

Both husband and wife are too well known to readers of Mme de Sévigné to make further description of them necessary. But I will quote some sentences from Saint-Simon's extremely fair notice, which was written after the death of Coulanges in 1716 at the age of eighty-two:

C'étoit un très-petit homme, gros à face rejouie[3] de ces esprits faciles, gais, agréables, qui ne produisent que de jolies bagatelles, mais qui en produisent toujours et de nouvelles et sur-le-champ [he was known as Le Chansonnier] léger, frivole, à qui ne coûtoit que la contrainte et l'étude, et dont tout étoit naturel....Il jamais ne dit mal ni ne fit mal à personne, et fut avec estime et amitié l'amusement et les délices de l'élite de son temps....Sa femme qui avoit plus d'esprit que lui, et qui l'avoit plus solide, eut aussi quantité d'amis à la ville et la cour où elle ne mettoit jamais le pied. [Both these remarks apply to her later years, after her illness in 1694, when she became devout and lived much in

[1] 15 to 21 December 1670.
[2] 22 July 1671. See above, p. 4.
[3] This well describes the portrait of the Hôtel de Carnavalet.

retirement.] Ils vivoient ensemble dans une grande union, mais avec des dissonances qui en faisoient le sel et qui rejouissoient toutes leur sociétés.... Elle avoit été fort jolie, mais toujours sage et considérée.[1]

It must be remembered that Saint-Simon was not presented at Court till 1691 when he was barely seventeen. Whether, if he had known Mme de Coulanges in her earlier years, he would have said that she was "toujours sage" is a question. I believe he would, for though she had three adorers—her cousin La Trousse, Brancas and the Abbé Têtu—and though she accepted their adoration, one gets the impression from Mme de Sévigné's letters, and especially from her relations with her husband, that she remained *sage*.

But before leaving M. de Coulanges I must quote two passages from Mme de Sévigné's letters to complete the picture. The first was written on 11 April 1685:

Je viens d'écrire au petit Coulanges: ma fantaisie étoit de le prêcher sur sa mauvaise petite conscience, dont il ne fait tous les ans que diminuer la quantité, craignant toujours la plénitude, sans jamais ôter de la qualité; car je suis assurée qu'au bout de la semaine[2] à Basville, son unique pêché, qui est *gaudeamus*, sera tout aussi bien établi chez lui qu'auparavant.

The second was written to Coulanges himself on 8 February 1690, when he was at Rome with the Duc de Chaulnes:

Toujours aimé, toujours estimé, toujours portant la joie et le plaisir avec vous, toujours favori et entête de quelque ami d'importance, un duc, un prince; un pape

---

[1] *Mémoires*, ed. Chéruel, XII, 416 f.
[2] Holy Week; Easter in 1685 was on 22 April.

(car j'y veux ajouter le saint-père pour la rareté), toujours en santé, jamais à charge à personne, point d'affaires, point d'ambition; mais surtout quel avantage de
ne point vieillir! voilà le comble du bonheur.

The whole letter is charming.

It was Mme de Sévigné's custom, as we have seen,
to dine every Friday with M. Lavardin de Beaumanoir,
the Bishop of Le Mans, and his widowed sister-in-law,
Mme de Lavardin. The Bishop died in July 1671, but
the dinners continued and Mme de Lavardin was one
of the chief sources of the news that Mme de Sévigné
retailed to her daughter. Twenty years later in a letter
to Coulanges she speaks of her as "mon intime et mon
ancienne amie". She was then seriously ill, and though
she lived for another three years she never recovered
her health and became childish. She was apparently
older than Mme de Sévigné, perhaps by six years.
Mme de Sévigné greatly valued her "bon et solide
esprit", but she was imperious and liked to have her
own way and to keep to her own hours and habits.
When her son became engaged to Mlle de Noailles,
sister of the Maréchal de Noailles, she wrote to Mme de
Sévigné that she was pleased. But she was not, says
Mme de Sévigné: "Une belle fille la dérange; je ne crois
pas qu'elles logent ensemble." However, Mme de
Mouci, who was a great friend of both ladies and had an
almost magical influence over Mme de Lavardin, persuaded her into a better humour and induced her to act
with greater liberality towards her son than she had at
first proposed. She told Mme de Sévigné that she would
die of laughter to see Mme de Lavardin's convulsions,

"when she exorcised and drove out of her the demon of avarice".[1]

Mme de Mouci herself was a most generous and unselfish woman. When her brother, Achille de Harlay, was made First President of the Paris *Parlement*, she gave him, in view of his increased expenses in entertaining, twelve thousand francs worth of silver plate and soon afterwards a fine piece of tapestry valued at two thousand pistoles, or twenty thousand francs.[2] In one of her letters Mme de Sévigné says that "the only advantage that Mme de Mouci seems to seek for herself is that of being the most admirable and the most romantic person in the world".[3] Saint-Simon, under the influence of prejudice, says that "she was stuck-up (*guindée*), affected, and religious by profession *avec tous les apanages de ce métier*", and complains that she left all her money to hospitals. But he is prejudiced by his hatred for her brother, whom he believed to have shewn gross partiality to the Duc de Luxembourg in his case against his brother *ducs et pairs*. His two portraits of him are in consequence masterpieces of finished malignancy, and those of Mme de Mouci, though only slight sketches, reflect the same prejudice.[4] Very likely, also, Saint-Simon who, though *dévot* with a perfectly genuine piety, disliked Mme de Mouci's tendency to mysticism.

A much older friend than Mme de Mouci, though she is not mentioned in Mme de Sévigné's letters earlier

---

[1] See letters of 9 and 12 June 1680.
[2] Letters of 9 and 19 October 1689.
[3] 30 June 1680.
[4] I, 137; V, 166.

than 1669, was Mme d'Huxelles,[1] daughter of Président Bailleul, Surintendant des Finances. She was born in the same year (1626) as Mme de Sévigné and having married, first, the Marquis de Nangis, and secondly the Marquis d'Huxelles, was left a widow for the second time in 1658. Both her husbands were killed at Gravelines, the former in 1644 and the latter on the eve of receiving a marshal's baton. Saint-Simon has two notices of her in much the same terms. This is what he wrote after her death in 1712:

C'étoit une femme de beaucoup d'esprit, qui avoit eu de la beauté et de la galanterie, qui savoit et qui avoit été du grand monde toute sa vie, mais point de la cour. Elle étoit impérieuse, et s'étoit acquis un droit d'autorité. Des gens d'esprit et de lettres et des vieillards de l'ancienne cour s'assembloient chez elle, où elle soutenoit une sorte de tribunal fort décisif. Elle conserva des amis et de la considération jusqu'au bout ! Son fils, qu'elle traite toujours avec hauteur, ne fut jamais trop bien avec elle, et ne la voyait guère.[2]

What Saint-Simon says of her *galanterie* is, so far as one can judge from contemporary mentions of her, a true indictment, but in 1669, when her eldest son was mortally wounded before Candia in the vain attempt to assist the Venetians against the Turks, she turned to religion, as her friend Mme de Longueville had done many years before. She made friends with Port-Royal,

[1] E. de Barthélemy, *La Marquise d'Huxelles et ses amis* 1881, a book which gives much interesting information about French society in the seventeenth century, and prints a good many letters from and to Mme d'Huxelles. Mme de Sévigné always writes her name Uxelles.

[2] IX, 299, and see *ib*. III, 384 for an earlier notice.

and the death of the Abbess, Mère Agnès, in 1671, seems greatly to have affected her. The first time that she is mentioned in Mme de Sévigné's letters is in August 1669, with reference to the death of her son, but from this time onwards they were frequently in one another's company. Mme d'Huxelles had a perfect mania for collecting and imparting news, and largely for this purpose corresponded with many distinguished persons. Her most frequent correspondent was the Marquis de La Garde, a cousin of M. de Grignan, who had an estate in Provence, and, as she kept him posted with the latest news of Paris and the Court and political affairs, it sometimes happened that Mme de Grignan got the news in this way earlier than she did from her mother. This evidently sometimes piqued Mme de Sévigné,[1] and as after January 1690 she never mentions Mme d'Huxelles in her letters Barthélemy conjectures that the friendship cooled down. Mme d'Huxelles survived her friend by sixteen years, dying at the age of eighty-five in 1712. She kept up her correspondence with the faithful La Garde till the end, and on the very day of her death her secretary wrote to him that, if he did not hear from her on the following Monday, it would be a bad sign.[2]

What Saint-Simon tells us of her relations with her surviving son is borne out by Mme de Sévigné, who, after remarking that she shewed very little joy at his

[1] See letters of 14 January and 28 August 1689.

[2] Three volumes of her letters to La Garde are preserved in the library of the Musée Calvet at Avignon. They contain letters from 1704–1705, 1709–1710, 1711–1712. Barthélemy prints several in an appendix.

receiving a slight wound at Philippsburg, which would bring him home, adds: "Ils ne sont ni parents ni amis."[1] In his mother's lifetime he became a distinguished soldier and received a marshal's baton. Saint-Simon, who was for a short time his colleague in the Council of Regency, evidently detested him. But even if we allow for prejudice in the portrait that he draws of him, which is even blacker than that of President de Harlay,[2] we cannot blame his mother for her attitude towards him.

I have now mentioned five woman-friends of Mme de Sévigné of whom the last three, Mme de Lavardin, Mme de Mouci, and Mme d'Huxelles, were widows and to whom she often refers as "les bonnes veuves". Later she added to them, with brevet rank, Mlle de La Rochefoucauld. This was probably the eldest of La Rochefoucauld's three daughters, who lived together in a corner of their father's *hôtel*. Saint-Simon says that she had "beaucoup d'esprit", and he also tells us—"ce qui est prodigieux"—that she was secretly married to Gourville, her father's former *maître d'hôtel*, and that all the family and nearly all the world knew of it but that no one who saw them together would ever have suspected it.[3]

It is just possible that Mme de Vins was one of the "five or six friends" referred to in the letter to Bussy, but it is not very probable, for Mme de Sévigné first made her acquaintance in December 1673, when she was Mlle Ladvocat. She met her on two occasions at

[1] 1 October 1688.   [2] *Mémoires*, III, 383–387.
[3] III, 422. For Gourville see below, pp. 68–69.

the house of her brother-in-law, M. de Pomponne, and says that she was "fort jolie et très-aimable" and that she added greatly to the pleasure of their conversations.[1] In the following year she married Jean de La Garde, Marquis de Vins, a Provençal and a cousin of the Comte de Grignan. After her marriage she still spent much of her time at Pomponne, where Mme de Sévigné often met her and took a great liking to her. It was in her favour no doubt that she was a friend and correspondent of Mme de Grignan. "Son amitié m'est aussi convenable que son âge me l'est peu: mais son esprit est si bon et si solide, qu'on peut la tenir pour vieille à cet endroit."[2] She was at that time studying Descartes at Pomponne. Saint-Simon, who was educated with her son, praises her *esprit*, her grace, her beauty and her virtue. The son, an only son, who was "handsome, amiable, and intelligent, like his mother", was killed in his first campaign at the battle of Steenkerke in 1692, when he could not have been more than seventeen. Saint-Simon says that the parents were never consoled, especially the poor mother, who retired from the world and "became absorbed for the rest of her life in her grief and her piety".[3] In the very last letter that we have of Mme de Sévigné's she refers to her friend's loss.[4]

Another intimate and older friend was Mme de La Troche, but as she did not settle permanently in Paris till 1675, she is certainly not to be included in the

[1] 8 and 11 December 1673.
[2] 13 October 1679. See also letters of 30 June and 3 July 1680.
[3] *Mémoires*, II, 250.   [4] 29 March 1696.

"five or six". Her husband was a Councillor of the Parliament of Rennes, so that it was no doubt in Brittany that Mme de Sévigné made her acquaintance. The friendship was occasionally interrupted by gusts of unreasonable jealousy on the part of *la Trochanire*, as Mme de Sévigné and her daughter called her. Thus Mme de Sévigné writes:

Je ne vous parle guère de Madame de la Troche; c'est que les flots de la mer ne sont plus agités que son procédé avec moi; elle est contente et mal contente dix fois par semaine, et cette diversité compose un désagrément incroyable dans la société: cette préférence du fauxbourg[1] est un point à quoi il est difficile de remédier: je suis aimée autant qu'on y peut aimer: la compagnie y est sûrement bonne; je ne suis contrebande à rien; ce qu'on y est une fois, on l'est toujours: de plus, notre Cardinal m'y donne souvent les rendez-vous; que faire à tout cela? En un mot je rénonce à plaire à Madame de la Troche, sans renoncer à l'aimer, car elle me trouvera toujours, quand elle voudra se faire justice.[2]

As Mme de Sévigné says in her next letter,[3] Mme de La Troche could not do without her and her coldness soon melted. She was in reality a most good-natured woman, who spared herself no trouble to oblige her friends: "Elle est toujours la bonté même, et allante et venante: on dit qu'elle est la femelle de d'Hacqueville."[4] She felt Mme de Sévigné's death deeply. Eight days afterwards—she died on 17 April 1696—when the news had just reached Paris, Coulanges writes to

[1] The Faubourg Saint-Germain, where both La Rochefoucauld and Mme de La Fayette lived.
[2] 15 April 1672.
[3] 20 April.   [4] 22 April 1676.

41

Pauline (Mme de Simiane) that he and his wife and the Duchesse de Chaulnes and Mme de La Troche met together to weep and to regret all that they had lost.[1]

The Duchesse de Chaulnes, like her fellow-mourner, was closely connected with Brittany, for her husband was governor of that province for twenty-six years. He was appointed in 1669, but in 1671, when Mme de Sévigné went to Les Rochers for the first time since his appointment, she was evidently on terms of intimate friendship with Mme de Chaulnes.[2] One of her letters describes how the latter arrived suddenly one day, saying that she could not be any longer without seeing her, and that the burden of Brittany on her shoulders was killing her. Then she flung herself on Mme de Sévigné's bed and slept from sheer fatigue, while the rest of the company went on with their conversation. When she had woken up, they all went for a walk and sat down in the woods, and while the others played at mall she gave an account to Mme de Sévigné of her life at Rome, where her husband had been sent as ambassador extraordinary for the conclaves of Clement IX (1667) and Clement X (1670), and of how she came to marry the Duke. A sudden downfall of rain put an end to their conversation and the whole company, wet to the skin, ran to the house, where Mme de Sévigné provided dry clothes, and they nearly died of laughter: "Voilà comme fut traitée la gouvernante de Bretagne dans son propre gouvernement."[3]

[1] 25 April 1696. [2] See letter of 26 July 1671.
[3] 23 August 1671.

In 1689 the Duc de Chaulnes was sent again to Rome, this time for the conclave of Alexander VIII (Cardinal Ottoboni), an old gentleman of eighty, favourable to France, whom, as Mme de Sévigné puts it, M. de Chaulnes made Pope on 6 October 1689. His diplomatic services and still more his work as governor of Brittany are beyond my present purport, but I will quote Saint-Simon's life-like portrait:

C'étoit sous la corpulence, l'épaisseur, la pesanteur, la physionomie d'un bœuf, l'esprit le plus délié, le plus délicat, le plus souple, le plus adroit à prendre et à pousser ses avantages, avec tout l'agrément et la finesse possible, jointes à une grande capacité et à une continuelle expérience de toutes sortes d'affaires, et la réputation de la plus exacte probité, décorée à l'extérieur d'une libéralité et d'une magnificence également splendide, et de beaucoup de dignité avec beaucoup de politesse.[1]

And here is the companion picture of Mme de Chaulnes, which is even better:

C'étoit, pour la figure extérieure, un soldat aux gardes, et même un peu suisse, habillé en femme: elle en avoit le ton et la voix, et des mots du bas peuple; beaucoup de dignité, beaucoup d'amis, une politesse choisie, un sens et un désir d'obliges qui tenoient lieu d'esprit, sans jamais rien de déplacé, une grande vertu, une libéralité naturelle et noble, avec beaucoup de magnificence, et tout le maintien, les façons, l'état et la réalité d'une grande dame en quelque lieu qu'elle se trouvât, comme M. de Chaulnes l'avoit de même d'un fort grand seigneur. Elle étoit, comme lui, adorée

[1] I, 170.

en Bretagne et fut pour le moins aussi sensible que lui
à l'échange forcé de gouvernement.[1]

The "forced exchange of government" was imposed
by Louis XIV, who wanted Brittany for his bastard,
the Comte de Toulouse, and offered M. de Chaulnes
Guyenne in exchange. The latter, says Saint-Simon,
left the King's cabinet with tears in his eyes, but he had
to obey. The Duchess was even more enraged than her
husband, and the Bretons were in despair.[2] The popularity of the Duke and Duchess in the province is amply
attested by Mme de Sévigné: "Ils ont senti", she writes,
"les vives douleurs de toute une Province qu'ils ont
gouvernée et comblée de biens depuis vingt-six ans."[3]
M. de Chaulnes died in September 1698—of grief, says
Saint-Simon, at the forced exchange of his government[4]—and his widow, who was inconsolable, followed him at the beginning of the next year. As they
left no children, Chaulnes went to his cousin the Duc de
Chevreuse, Fénelon's great friend,[5] and thus gave its
name to the plan of government—*Tables de Chaulnes*—
which Chevreuse and Fénelon drew up in concert in
1711.

An old friend of Mme de Sévigné who also did
good service for Louis XIV was Henri de Daillon, Duc
du Lude, a distinguished soldier who was made a
duc et pair in 1675. He already held the post of Grand
Master of the Artillery, with the Arsenal for his official

---

[1] *Mémoires*, II, 169 f. [2] *Mémoires*, II, pp. 232–234.
[3] 26 April 1695. [4] *Mémoires*, III, pp. 103 f.
[5] With survival to his second son, the Vidame d'Amiens who
became, by the creation of a new *duché-pairie*, Duc de Chaulnes.
He married a granddaughter of Mme de Lavardin.

residence. He was one of Mme de Sévigné's admirers in her early widowhood and she always held him in high esteem. He had a reputation as a wit and was a notable figure in the social world. His first wife died, and in 1681 he married the beautiful widow of the Comte de Guiche. She was a Béthune by birth, a great-niece of Henri IV's minister. Born about 1640 she married in 1658 the Comte de Guiche, that brilliant ornament of the Court of Louis XIV, the announcement of whose premature death in 1673 to his father the Duc de Gramont by Bourdaloue is told so touchingly by Mme de Sévigné. The marriage was an unhappy one, for Guiche had many love-affairs, including a passion for Mme Henriette,[1] and neglected his wife. After his death Mme de Sévigné reports her as saying:

Il étoit aimable, je l'aurois aimé passionément s'il m'avoit un peu aimée; j'ai souffert ses mépris avec douleur; sa mort me touche et me fait pitié; j'espérois toujours qu'il changeroit de sentiment pour moi.[2]

Her second marriage was a happy one, but it was childless and it only lasted four years, for the Duc du Lude died in 1685, leaving his widow immensely rich with the wealth of both her husbands. She was, says Saint-Simon, "toujours sage, sans aucun esprit que celui qui donne l'usage du grand monde et le désir

---

[1] See Mme de La Fayette, *Henriette d'Angleterre*. She speaks of him as "le jeune homme de la cour le plus beau et le mieux fait, aimable de sa personne, galant, hardi, brave, rempli de grandeur et d'élévation. La vanité...et un air méprisant... ternissaient un peu tout ce mérite."

[2] 8 December 1673.

de plaire à tout le monde".[1] Mme de Sévigné evidently continued with her her old friendship for her husband. She was still beautiful, notes Saint-Simon, in 1694, when she was past fifty, and even ten years later Mme de Coulanges, after a four days' visit from her, writes to Mme de Grignan that it is ridiculous to be so beautiful—"les années coulent sur elle, comme l'eau sur la toile cirée". In 1696 she was appointed *dame d'honneur* to the young Duchesse de Bourgogne and became in high favour with the Court, and especially with the King. Her mother, Mme de Verneuil, is not often mentioned in Mme de Sévigné's letters, but she was an old and valued friend. She married, first the Duc de Sully, and secondly in 1668 the Duc de Verneuil, son of Henri IV by Henriette d'Entragues, who, without ever being even in deacon's orders, had held the bishopric of Metz for fifty-nine years. He was sixty-seven when she married him and in 1682 she became a widow for the second time. Mme du Lude was her daughter by her first husband.

Another friend of Mme de Sévigné who rose to eminence in the King's service was Paul Barillon, son of a Président d'Enquêtes. He entered diplomacy, and in 1671 was sent to England. Here he served first under Courtin and then as ambassador in 1677. His dispatches from December 1684 to the following December are of considerable importance as shewing the policy of his master with regard to James II. It is a stroke of irony that the encouragement which Louis XIV gave to James to further Roman Catholic interests was

[1] I, 337.

the main cause of his deposition and of the fatal effect which it had on the French King's ambitious schemes.[1] Barillon resigned his post early in 1689 and returned to Paris where Mme de Sévigné reports him as "fort gros" and "ravi de retrouver ses vieilles amies. Il est souvent chez Mme de La Fayette et Mme de Coulanges."[2] And a little later she writes:

M. de Barillon est riche, gros, *vieux*, à ce qu'il dit, et regarde sans envie la brillante place de M. d'Avaux [his successor]. Il aime la paix et la tranquillité au milieu de ses amis et de sa famille.[3]

Yet another old friend, and a very intimate one, was Simon Arnauld, Marquis de Pomponne, second son of Arnauld d'Andilly, who took his title after his marriage with Catherine Ladvocat. Everyone knows the letters in which Mme de Sévigné in November and December 1664 kept him informed about the trial of Foucquet. He, too, was a friend of Foucquet and on that account had been exiled to Verdun. But in the following year he was allowed to return and was sent as ambassador to Stockholm, then to the Hague, and then back to Stockholm. From this last post he was recalled in 1671 to succeed Lyonne as Foreign Minister. He held the office till 1679 when, largely owing to the intrigues of Colbert and Louvois, and partly because he was too honourable to give a firm support to Louis's policy of "clandestine annexation", he was dismissed in disgrace. But four months

[1] In 1687 Barillon reported truly to Louis XIV on the real state of feeling in the country. See Macaulay, *Works*, II, 106.
[2] 21 and 22 January 1689.   [3] 21 March 1689.

later he was recalled to Court and on Louvois's death in 1691 Louis XIV at once reappointed him to the *Conseil d'État*. He became on excellent terms with Croissy, the Foreign Secretary, and when that minister died in 1696 and was succeeded by his son Torcy, Pomponne assisted the latter, who was his son-in-law, in the conduct of foreign affairs. He had never been ill in his life, but at the age of eighty-one a meal of cold veal and peaches carried him off in four days (1699).

Saint-Simon's portrait of Pomponne, who was an intimate friend of his father, is a striking refutation of the opinion that the great memoir-writer's portraits are always unfavourable. He speaks of him as a diplomatist and a foreign minister in the very highest terms, and he ends by saying: "La douceur et le sel de son commerce étoient charmants, et ses conversations, sans qu'il le voulût, infiniment instructives."[1] Mme de Sévigné's opinion of him was equally high. In a letter to her daughter written the day after her first meeting with him after his return from Sweden she says:

Il faudroit plus de papier qu'il n'y en a dans mon cabinet, pour vous dire la joie que nous avions de nous revoir....Enfin, je ne l'ai point trouvé changé; il est toujours parfait. Il me donne toujours de l'esprit; le sien est tellement aisé, qu'on prend, sans y penser, une confiance qui fait qu'on parle heureusement de tout ce qu'on pense.[2]

Nearly twenty years later she writes of the joy with which she had heard of his return to the ministry, and

[1] I, 243–250.   [2] 3 February 1672.

with what general approbation it had been greeted.[1]
With his father, Robert Arnauld, she was on equally
affectionate terms. I have already recounted the visit
that she paid to him in April 1671, when he was staying
at Pomponne while his son was absent in Sweden, and
of the six hours of very agreeable, but very serious, conversation that she had with him. The serious feature
was that he had reproached her with idolising her
daughter, saying that this kind of idolatry was as
dangerous as any other and that she was a pretty
pagan.[2] Though he was staying at Pomponne his real
home at this time was the farm of Les Granges, where
Les MM. de Port-Royal, whom he had joined in 1646,
had retired, when the nuns returned to their original
home. In a letter of September of the same year she
records a conversation which "le bon homme", as
she always calls him, had with the King just after he
had appointed Pomponne to be his Foreign Minister.[3]
The old man died in 1674 at the age of eighty-six.

In October 1685 Mme de Sévigné writes to Bussy
that she has just been staying with M. de Lamoignon
at Basville (near Versailles), where she found her
daughter and "all the Grignans": "Il y a longtemps
que je n'avois eu une plus parfaite joie." For she had
been at Les Rochers since the previous September,
while her daughter was in Paris, and therefore had not
seen her for more than a year. Bourdaloue and Rapin
were also of the party.[4] Chrétien-François de Lamoignon, eldest son of Guillaume de Lamoignon, the dis-

[1] 14 August 1691.   [3] 27 April 1671.
[2] 23 September 1671.   [4] 5 October 1683.

tinguished First President of the *Parlement* of Paris,[1] was Advocate-General when Mme de Sévigné stayed with him—a post which he held for twenty-five years (1673–1698) with general approval. "C'étoit un homme enivré de la cour," says Saint-Simon, "de la faveur du grand et brillant monde, qui se vouloit mêler de tous les mariages et tous les testaments, et à qui, comme à tout Lamoignon, il ne se falloit fier que de bonne sorte." Like his father before him he was fond of entertaining men-of-letters, both at his country-house of Basville and at his Paris *hôtel*, which, dating from the time of Henri III, was situated in the Rue Pavée at the corner of the Rue Neuve Sainte-Catherine, just opposite to the garden of the Hôtel de Carnavalet. Among the more frequent guests were Boileau, Racine, Bourdaloue, and Rapin. It was at one of these dinners that the famous scene between Boileau and a Jesuit father, who had accompanied Bourdaloue, took place.[1] Boileau's Sixth Epistle is addressed to Lamoignon.[2] He was evidently on friendly terms both with the Grignan family and Mme de Sévigné, but the first time that we hear of him in her letters is in one of 29 November 1684, in which she refers to her daughter meeting him and his wife in Paris, and says, "Oh! pour celui-là, il devoit vous faire oublier votre écriture et votre écritoire", which seems to imply that he was a great talker.

---

[1] He is best known as having forbidden the representation of *Tartuffe* in 1667. Molière had an interview with him: but, though extremely polite, he was quite firm.

[2] See below, pp. 128–129.

When Mme de Sévigné was staying at Basville, an expected guest was Jean Corbinelli, who throughout her correspondence makes frequent appearances as an intimate and trusted friend: "Vous savez comme Corbinelli m'est bon, et de quelle sorte il entre dans mes sentiments. Je suis convaincu de son amitié, je sens son absence," and three weeks later: "Il m'aime fort, je l'aime aussi." He was of a Florentine family, allied both to the Medici and the Gondi. His grandfather, a man of considerable learning, had come to France as an exile and had been appointed by Catherine de' Medici tutor to her son, the future Henri III. Mme de Sévigné's friend was popular in society and had a considerable reputation as a critic and a wit. He was a friend of Bussy, with whom he frequently corresponded. From time to time he published little volumes of extracts from celebrated writers, but his chief work was a *Histoire généalogique de la maison de Gondi*. He was an admirer and student of Descartes and late in life he was attracted to mysticism and to the *Pratique facile* of Malaval, which had been recently put on the Index. Mme de Grignan called his mysticism *Le mystique du diable* and evidently did not like him.[1] But she was jealous of most of her mother's friends, notably of Mme de La Fayette. Evidently Mme de Sévigné dwells on Corbinelli's virtues partly in the hope of overcoming her daughter's dislike. He died, a centenarian, in 1716.

Mme de Sévigné and Corbinelli had a common friend in M. de Moulceau, President of the Chambre

[1] Letters of 11 September 1689 and 15 January 1690.

des Comptes at Montpellier, where she made his acquaintance, probably during her first visit to Grignan (July to October 1672). Her letters to him were first published in 1773 together with the letters of her granddaughter, Mme de Simiane. They range from 26 November 1681 to 29 February 1696, seven weeks before her death. They include a few letters from Corbinelli and there are interpolations by him in some of Mme de Sévigné's. He also made the President's acquaintance at Montpellier, where he was imprisoned for a time in company with his friend and patron, that accomplished favourite of society and professional seducer, the Marquis de Vardes, and where he often visited his friend during his eighteen years of exile. Mme de Sévigné valued M. de Moulceau's friendship highly. "Adieu, le plus amiable ami du monde",[1] she writes in one letter, and in another she says:

J'aime votre esprit, votre mérite, votre sagesse, votre folie, votre vertu, votre humeur, votre bonté, enfin, tout ce qui est en vous.[2]

There is just a little stiffness, foreign to Mme de Sévigné, in the two earliest letters, and in the second she apologises for the obscurity of a sentence with the words: "Mettez-la sur le compte du pompeux galimatias que vous m'avez si bien inspiré." But in a rather later letter, in which she describes the return of Vardes from exile to the Court and his conversation with Louis XIV—all from hearsay—she is at her very best.[3] She is evidently on very good terms with her corre-

[1] 28 October 1682.   [2] 29 April 1682.   [3] 26 May 1682.

spondent, for she tells him not only the news from Paris—"J'aimerois mieux mourir qu'un autre vous eût mandé que le Prince de Conti est enfin revenu à la cour"—but also family news such as the marriage of her son in 1684 and of her grandson in 1695 and the death of the *bien Bon* in 1687.

An older friend was the celebrated Cardinal de Retz. When he died in 1679 she writes to Bussy that she had been his friend for thirty years and adds:

Je n'avois jamais reçu que des marques tendres de son amitié. Elle m'étoit également honorable et délicieuse. Il étoit d'un commerce aisé plus que personne au monde.[1]

Thirty years takes us back to the beginning of the Fronde, when M. de Sévigné was alive. It was no doubt through him that Mme de Sévigné became acquainted with Retz, who was his cousin. In 1662 Retz resigned his archbishopric and received in exchange, with other benefices, the abbey of Saint-Denis, but he had permission from the Pope to reside on his estate at Commercy in Lorraine. He did good service to France in three conclaves and he employed his leisure time in the virtuous task of paying his debts, and latterly in the less virtuous, but more amusing, one of writing his memoirs. Then in 1675 he was converted, and, as the result, he put the resignation of his Cardinal's hat in the hands of the Pope—an unheard-of step—he moved from Commercy to the Benedictine Abbey of Saint-Mihiel; and, greatest sacrifice of all, he abandoned his memoirs. But the Pope declared that

[1] 25 August 1679.

it was impossible to accept his resignation, and bade him go back to Commercy. Three years later he moved into his Abbey of Saint-Denis, and paid occasional visits to his great friends M. and Mme de Caumartin, who lived about twelve miles from Paris, or in Paris itself to his niece, the Duchesse de Lesdiguières. Mme de Sévigné was in constant relations with him, corresponding with him at Commercy and Rome, and visiting him when he was in Paris or the neighbour-hood. On 5 June 1675 she writes that she sees him every evening from eight to ten and that they talked unceasingly—this must be an exaggeration—about Mme de Grignan. She delighted in his conversation and his stories about his adventures, which, according to La Rochefoucauld, often owed more to his imagina-tion than to his memory. It is touching to note her solicitous care for his welfare and entertainment:

> Nous tâchons d'amuser notre bon Cardinal: Corneille lui a lu une pièce qui sera jouée dans quelques jours et qui fait souvenir des anciennes.[1] Molière lui lira samedi *Trissotin* [meaning *Les Femmes savantes*] qui est une fort plaisante chose. Despréaux lui donnera son *Lutrin* et sa *Poétique*.[2]

Like her contemporaries she greatly admired his strange proposal, which he made twice in 1675, that he should resign his rank as cardinal. It is difficult for readers of his memoirs to reconcile this rôle of penitence and piety with the political intrigues and scandalous love-affairs of his younger days, but it must be remembered, as Sainte-Beuve points out, that during the Fronde he

[1] See above, p. 120. [2] 3 March 1672.

fulfilled his duties as archbishop to the satisfaction of his flock, and kept his vices and weaknesses carefully in the background.[1] The Jansenists were particularly favourable to him. He was equally so to them, and he greatly esteemed "le grand Arnauld". It is not therefore so surprising as it seems at first sight that Mme de Sévigné and her friends should have looked upon him as a true penitent and as presenting in his retreat a beautiful example of devout and benign old age. One friend of Mme de Sévigné, however, did not share this view. La Rochefoucauld who, as we know, took a low view of human nature, ends his portrait of him with

La retraite qu'il vient de faire est la plus éclatante et la plus fausse action de sa vie; c'est un sacrifice qu'il fait à son orgueil, sous prétexte de dévotion; il quitte la Cour où il ne peut s'attacher, et il s'éloigne du monde qui s'éloigne de lui.[2]

Bussy was equally sceptical, but the majority of the Cardinal's contemporaries certainly believed in his sincerity. Saint-Simon who, though he was only a child at the time, must often have heard his father and others of that generation talk about him, seems to have had no doubt. He says simply: "Dieu l'a touché." Yet he

[1] *Causeries du Lundi*, v, 53 f. And see for Mme de Sévigné and the Cardinal, *ib*. pp. 252–254. These pages form part of two articles on Retz.

[2] The portrait was written for Mme de Sévigné, and not meant to be shewn to the Cardinal. She sent a copy to her daughter, saying that she thought it very good, and begged her to return it (Letter of 19 June 1675).

had read the memoirs, at least in the expurgated form in which they first appeared in 1717.[1]

Mme de Sévigné's affection for the Cardinal was perfectly genuine, but it was not wholly disinterested. This appears from a letter which she wrote to Mme de Grignan in May 1675 enclosing a letter for her from "notre cardinal" in which she says: "Être avec lui, et faire quelque chose pour vous, voilà ce qui m'est uniquement bon."[2] The enclosure for his "très-chère nièce"—she was his first cousin twice removed and therefore a niece à la mode de Bretagne—consisted only of four lines. As it turned out, the payment of his debts exhausted his estate, and he did not leave enough even for his funeral.

The Comte de Guitaut and his wife were old and intimate friends. At one time they lived close to Mme de Sévigné in the Rue de Thorigny, and their château at Époisses in Burgundy was not far from her ancestral home at Bourbilly, of which Guitaut was *seigneur*. We first hear of him in February 1671, when Mme de Sévigné in one of her best-known letters gives an extraordinarily vivid account of the fire which destroyed part of his house at Paris and which she witnessed from the window of her little grandchild's bedroom.[3] We next hear of him in 1673, when on her return from Provence she paid him a three days' visit at his château, which she found "d'une grandeur et d'une beauté sur-

[2] See for the whole question A. Gazier, *Les dernières années du Cardinal de Retz*, 1875. This ardent Jansenist has no doubt about Retz's sincerity. See also letters of 5 and 24 July 1675.

[2] Capmas, I, 336.

[3] 20 February 1671, known as the *Lettre de l'Incendie*.

prenantes".[1] Her next visit to Époisses was in August 1677, on her way to Vichy. She spent eight days there, and afterwards her host escorted her as far as Saulieu.[2] There is an interesting touch of self-revelation in the first of the letters in which she recounts this visit:

Nos conversations sont infinies; il aime à causer; et quand on me met en train, je ne fais pas mal aussi; de sorte qu'on ne peut pas être mieux ensemble que nous y sommes.

M. Guitaut was evidently, as she says, "very good company", and "nothing was so easy as to love him". The two evidently got on very well together, and before they parted at Saulieu they wrote to Mme de Grignan a joint letter full of humour and gaiety. In the days of the Fronde Guitaut had been a faithful supporter of Condé and in the battle at the gate of Saint-Antoine, like La Rochefoucauld, he was severely wounded.[3]

During his lifetime there are no letters addressed separately to Mme de Guitaut and only two or three to her conjointly with her husband. But Mme de Sévigné evidently had a real regard for her and after her husband's death in December 1685 they continued on terms of warm friendship. In a letter of 19 December 1688 she describes in a tone of devout admiration the Christian death of her uncle, M. de Saint-Aubin. In 1692 she begins a regular correspondence with her and there are thirty letters to her from that year till the end of 1694. They often take a serious tone, for Mme de

[1] 25 October 1673.
[2] 21, 25, 26 and 29 August 1677.
[3] Mlle de Montpensier, *Mémoires*, II, 97 f.

Guitaut was evidently a woman who thought much and intelligently on serious subjects.

Though he died as early as 1678, that is to say eighteen years before Mme de Sévigné, there are few names that occur more frequently in her correspondence than that of d'Hacqueville. He was at college with Retz and his devoted friend, and he helped largely to get him a pension of 6000 *livres*. His most endearing characteristic was that he was always ready to help his friends, sparing no labour to achieve his object. Mme de Sévigné frequently speaks of his kindness, but nowhere more strongly than in a letter of 18 December 1675 when he was helping the Grignans in an affair of some public importance:

> Je n'ai jamais vu des tons et des manières fermes et puissantes pour soutenir des amis, comme celles qu'il a: c'est un trésor de bonté, d'amitié et de capacité, à quoi il faut ajouter une application et une exactitude, dont nul autre que lui est capable.[1]

And four years earlier she had written:

> Cela fait plaisir au cœur de songer qu'on a un ami comme lui, à qui rien de bon, ni de solide ne manque, et qui ne nous peut jamais manquer lui-même.[2]

He gave help to so many friends at once that he seemed to be more than one man, and they called him *les d'Hacquevilles*, but, says Mme de Sévigné, "there is really no one in the world like our d'Hacqueville".[3] He had a mania for collecting news and for disseminating it to his friends not only by word of mouth but

[1] 18 December 1675.
[2] 17 April 1671.   [3] 8 December 1675.

in numerous letters. "Si vous aviez vu sa table", says Mme de Sévigné, "les mercredis, les vendredis, les samedis, vous croiriez être au bureau de la grand' poste." He sometimes wrote to her three times a week, and as his handwriting was very difficult to read this was not an unmixed blessing. "Il faudrait être dénaturée pour ne se pas crever les yeux à la déchiffrer", she says in one of her letters.

I have mentioned the Marquis de La Garde, the cousin of M. de Grignan, as Mme d'Huxelles's correspondent. His name often appears in Mme de Sévigné's letters, and as his property marched with that of his cousin, he was a connecting link between the two families. Mme de Grignan, however, felt coldly towards him, in spite of her mother's insistence on his good qualities. Indeed, at one time Mme de Sévigné herself was displeased with him and thought him wanting in generosity and gratitude, because he had refused to make a small loan to the Grignans.[2] But when she heard from her daughter that he was as badly off as they were, she completely changed her mind and declared that she had been foolish and unjust, and she adds:

Vous me dépeignez un véritable saint, une vertu toute chrétienne, et qui augmente infiniment l'estime que j'ai toujours eu pour lui,[3]

and a little later she says: "Je revère et j'honore et aime M. de La Garde." He died in 1713, leaving his château and estate to his niece *à la mode de Bretagne*, Mme de Simiane.

[1] 13 October 1680.   [2] 4 and 28 December 1689.
[3] 19 February 1690 (Capmas, II, 332).

Another friend of equally high character, though somewhat of an oddity, was the Abbé Têtu. This is how Saint-Simon speaks of him:

> Un homme fort singulier, qui étoit mêlé toute sa vie dans la meilleure compagnie de la ville, la cour, et de fort bonne compagnie lui-même.....Il primoit partout; on en rioit, mais on le laissoit faire. Il étoit très bon ami et serviable...simple, sans ambition, sans intérêt, bon homme et honnête homme, mais fort vif, fort dangéreux, et fort difficile à pardonner.[1]

He was a member of the Académie Française for more than forty years, though neither his verse, which included hymns, nor his prose is of much merit. According to Saint-Simon he was one of the first men to have the vapours and at one time they were so bad that he could not sleep even with the help of opium. Mme de Sévigné's letters in December 1688 and January 1689 are full of pity for him. In the bygone days he was the dominant figure at the Hôtel de Richelieu and aspired to be its Voiture. It was there that he met Mme Scarron and formed a life-long friendship with her. Her niece, Mme de Caylus, has left a portrait of him, which is much less favourable than Saint-Simon's. She says that he had a great idea of his own merit, that he could not bear contradiction—which agrees with Saint-Simon's "il primoit partout"—and that he was happiest when surrounded by a circle of admiring women. He was for a time one of Mme de Coulanges's adorers, having as rivals the Marquis de La Trousse, her husband's and Mme de Sévigné's first

[1] *Mémoires*, IV, 444 f.

cousin, and Charles, Comte de Brancas, a highly original character, who is often said to be the original of La Bruyère's *Ménalque*. But *Ménalque* is not so much an individual character as a collection of stories of absent-mindedness taken from several originals, of whom Brancas was one. Mme de Sévigné tells several good stories of him, but always with an affectionate sympathy, and a sincere regard for his disinterested character.[1] "Brancas m'a écrit une lettre excessivement tendre", she writes on 19 July 1691, and she adds: "Je lui faisois une réponse sur le même ton, ce seroit une *Portugaise*." This shews that she had read the *Lettres Portugaises*, published in 1669 and reprinted twenty times up to 1700.

When Mme de Sévigné went to Brittany for the first time after her daughter's marriage she was accompanied by her son, the Abbé de Coulanges, and the Abbé La Mousse. On the journey she writes that "La Mousse tient bien sa partie", and at Les Rochers she said that she and her son and he got on well together. She taught him Italian and read Tasso with him. Altogether, she found him an agreeable companion, and when she paid her first visit to Provence in July 1672 she again took him with her. He was somewhat alarmed at the prospect, as appears from the following passage:

La Mousse a été un peu ébranlé de la crainte des puces, des punaises, des scorpions, des chemins, et du bruit qu'il trouvera peut-être; tout cela lui faisoit un monstre dont je me suis bien moquée; et puis dire:

[1] See 21 April, 13 May and 10 June.

quelle figure! hélas! je ne sais rien, il y aura tant de monde: nous appellons cela des humilités glorieuses.[1]

On her next visit to Les Rochers—in the summer of 1675—La Mousse no longer formed one of the party: "Je ne veux point de la belle Mousse; l'ennui des autres me pèse plus que le mien."[2] And in April 1676 she writes that "il ne se communique guère; il est difficile à trouver, encore plus à conserver. Il est souvent mal content; il a eu une gronderie avec mon fils."[3] She mentions him again in September 1680, but evidently they became estranged. In one of the songs of the day he is referred to as the son (illegitimate) of M. de Gué-Bagnols, Mme de Coulanges's father. This is not very good evidence, but in a letter of 11 October 1688 Mme de Sévigné writes: "Le frère de Mme de Coulanges est mort", which can refer to no one else. It is true that it does not appear from this dry announcement that he had ever been a friend.

As for his fellow Abbé, Christophe de Coulanges, *le bien Bon*, who for fifty years, from the day that he became her guardian till his death, watched over his niece's interests with the tenderest vigilance, completing her education till she married, and after her husband's death managing her estates in Brittany and Burgundy with careful economy and a constant eye to her advantage, it is unnecessary to speak here. Moreover, in the next chapter, when we come to Livry and Les Rochers, where he was part of Mme de Sévigné's life, he will find inevitable mention. His one weakness,

[1] 8 July 1672.   [2] 28 June 1675.
[3] 22 April 1676.

except perhaps a too great love of building, at any rate for his niece's pocket, was his inability to resist the pleasures of the table. Before her first visit to Provence Mme de Sévigné begs her daughter not to go beyond her ordinary fare on their account:

Car si vous en mettez un pigeon davantage, nous le souffrirons pas; c'est le moyen de faire mourir notre Abbé que de le tenter de mangeaille.[1]

In a letter from Montpellier, where she paid a short visit in 1672, she says, "Le *bien Bon* mange comme un démon",[2] and five years later she writes from Vichy that he was drinking the waters "pour purger tous ses bons dîners".[3]

The Abbé de Coulanges had two brothers, both older than himself—Philippe, the father of *le petit* Coulanges, and Charles, Seigneur de Saint-Aubin—and one sister (besides Mme de Sévigné's mother), Henriette, widow of the Marquis de La Trousse and mother of Mme de Coulanges's adorer. She looked after the little Marie-Blanche, the Grignans's eldest daughter, when Mme de Sévigné was at Les Rochers in 1671, but at the beginning of the following year she was attacked by a severe illness which turned to dropsy. But she lingered on for some months, and Mme de Sévigné, though she was longing to start for Provence, would not leave her till the end came on the last day of June. Saint-Aubin is seldom mentioned in the letters. In 1679 we hear

[1] 8 July 1672.

[2] Capmas, I, 301. From an unpublished letter, headed, "Montpellier, samedi", to which Capmas assigns the date of 1 or 8 October 1672. The visit to Montpellier, unrecorded elsewhere, evidently took place about this time.

[3] 16 September 1677.

of him at Livry, where he found a mall, and proved to be a good player at the game.[1] But he is chiefly known to readers of Mme de Sévigné from her moving account of his Christian death nine years later in her letters to Mme de Guitaut and to her daughter.[2] The affectionate solicitude with which she soothed his last days, as she had done those of her aunt, is a testimony to her pious regard for the ties of relationship.

The same regard for family ties shews itself in her kindness to her cousin Mlle de Méri, the daughter of Mme de La Trousse. She required a great deal of attention, for she was an invalid and a valetudinarian, subject to feverish attacks and headaches. After her mother's death she lived alone in Mme de Sévigné's quarter. In spite of the trouble that her relations took to find her houses, she was always dissatisfied and she had trouble with her servants. Anxiety and worry brought on her nervous attacks, and in September and October of 1679 she was really ill.[3] At last after Easter 1680 she found a haven of refuge in the Hôtel de Carnavalet, where she occupied Mme de Grignan's own room[4] till the latter arrived in the following November for a visit which lasted nearly eight years. It does not appear, however, that Mlle de Méri left the *hôtel* altogether. At any rate we find her there eight years later, when Mme de Sévigné writes that "Made-

[1] 6 October 1679.

[2] See above, p. 57, for the first; I shall refer to the second in my next chapter.

[3] See letters of 15 September, 16 and 24 November, 1 and 31 December 1679, and Capmas, II, 49, 74 and 122.

[4] 12 April 1680 (Capmas, II, 134) and 26 April 1680.

moiselle de Méri se trouve bien de nous, et nous d'elle".[1]

Mme de Sévigné's connexion with that Hôtel de Carnavalet which is for ever associated with her name, began on 1 October 1677, when she took a lease of it for three years. Before this she had been living first in the Rue Thorigny and then in the Rue Courteau-Vilain, where she moved in May 1672.[2] The Hôtel de Carnavalet was in the Rue Culture-Sainte-Catherine des Filles Bleues (now the Rue de Sévigné), which runs into the Rue de Rivoli almost opposite to the Church of Saint-Paul. Thus she never lived much more than a quarter of a mile from the Place Royale (now Place des Vosges), where she was born.

Her new house, which she describes in a letter of 12 October 1677,[3] was a large one, for it was destined to provide accommodation for the Grignan family, including M. de Grignan's two daughters by his first wife and Mme de Grignan's confidential attendant, Mlle de Montgobert. The arrangement of the rooms was first made by d'Hacqueville, and adopted with some modifications by Mme de Sévigné. There was a coach-house for four carriages and stalls for eighteen horses. And there was a large garden. The removal began when Mme de Sévigné returned from Vichy on 7 October, and she first slept in her new home soon after 22 October. At any rate on 22 October[4] she was still staying with the Coulanges, who had taken her in during the removal. We get an interesting picture of

[1] 18 October 1688. [2] See Capmas, II, 79, n. 4.
[3] *Ib.* 15 ff. [4] Letter of that date.

how her friends came to visit her while she was super-intending the work—sometimes in the court, where they sat on the pole of her coach.[1] Early in November the Grignans arrived to find everything in order. Their visit lasted a year and ten months. The next visit of Mme de Grignan was for a much longer period, for she was there from November 1680 to October 1688. When the Grignan family were not at Paris Mme de Sévigné often used their apartments for her friends, who seem to have been in the position of more or less independent lodgers rather than of boarders or what are now called paying guests. We have seen that Mlle de Méri was living there in 1680, and again in 1688, just after Mme de Grignan's long visit. About the same time came the Abbé Bigorre, who, as I have said, succeeded d'Hacqueville as an indefatigable collector of news. Mme de Sévigné writes on 18 October 1688 that she found him the most accommodating and amiable of guests, and again a fortnight later that he is the best friend and the most amiable guest that one could wish for. In the same letter she says that Mlle de Méri was occupying Mme de Grignan's room and that the Chevalier de Grignan was also staying there.[2] From Corbinelli's interpolations in Mme de Sévigné's letters, especially in those to M. de Moulceau, it is evident that he was often there either as a lodger or a visitor. The interpolations occur in letters of various dates from November 1679 to March 1689, and in that of 2 March 1689 he says definitely, " Je demeure à l'hôtel de Carna-valet."

[1] 20 October 1677.   [2] 2 November 1688.

In the last paragraph I mentioned the Chevalier de Grignan. He was the youngest brother of the Comte de Grignan and the only one with whom Mme de Sévigné was on terms of intimacy and affection. In the earlier letters he appears as a soldier of great promise, much esteemed by Turenne. But, while still quite young, he began to be tormented with gout and in 1680 he had to retire from service with a pension and was made a *Menin*, or gentleman-in-waiting, to the Dauphin. He must have come to the Hôtel de Carnavalet in 1688 almost immediately after the Grignans's departure, for on 8 October Mme de Sévigné writes that he was suffering badly from the gout and bearing it heroically. Three months later he was well enough to be present at a supper which Mme de Coulanges gave for her gouty friends. Other guests were M. and Mme de Lamoignon, the Abbé de Marsillac, Mme de Sévigné, who had had rheumatism twelve years previously, and *le petit* Coulanges, who, though he had hitherto escaped the gout, "deserved to have it". He did in fact have it less than a month later.[1] At this party he sang his own songs and gave special pleasure to the Abbé de Marsillac, who expressed his approval with gestures which recalled those of his father, La Rochefoucauld. There were two other guests, Mme de Frontenac and her inseparable friend, Mlle d'Outrelaise, both great friends of Mme de Coulanges and known to everybody as *Les Divines*.[2] Mme de Frontenac, who, in the words of Saint-Simon, was "extrêmement du grand monde et du plus recherché", was the wife of

[1] 4 February 1689.   [2] 10 January 1689.

the Comte de Frontenac, that remarkable man who was Governor of Canada from 1672 to 1682 and again from 1689 till his death in 1698. His wife did not accompany him to Canada but lived with Mlle d'Outrelaise in the Arsenal in an apartment which the Duc du Lude gave her when he was Grand Master.[1]

This supper-party may be taken as a good example of the friendly and informal way in which Mme de Sévigné and her friends dined or supped together. Even to a grander supper-party, which was given by that popular Amphitryon, Gourville, Mme de Sévigné was only invited "avec toutes sortes d'amitié", on the same evening. Sainte-Beuve, in a *causerie* on this remarkable man, calls him a superior Gil-Blas,[2] but emphasis must be laid on the word "superior". Born on the La Rochefoucauld estates, he began life as valet[3] to the Abbé de La Rochefoucauld, afterwards Bishop of Lectoure. Transferred to the service of the eldest brother, the writer of the *Maximes*, he became first his house-steward and then his secretary, and served under him (with discretion) during the Fronde. This brought him into close relations with Condé. After the Fronde he entered by the advice of Mazarin into finance, and enriched himself first by legitimate, and then under Foucquet by illegitimate means. Involved in the latter's downfall he was condemned to death, fled from France and for eight years led a wandering life in various

[1] See Saint-Simon, *Mémoires*, II, 192 and v, 122.
[2] *Causeries du Lundi*, v, 358 ff.
[3] "Sosie de la livrée a passé, par une petite recette, à une sous-ferme" (La Bruyère, *Des biens de fortune*). He probably has Gourville in mind.

countries of Europe. In 1671 he returned to Paris, got his sentence revoked, and made himself useful to Condé, to whom La Rochefoucauld had practically transferred him. He was also on familiar terms with Colbert, Louvois, and Lyonne, rendering service to all of them by his remarkable tact in diplomatic negotiations and his peculiar skill in intrigue. In fact his power of making himself useful to great men and of winning their confidence was phenomenal. But he never lost sight of the interests of his patrons La Rochefoucauld and Condé.[1]

The other guests, besides Mme de Sévigné, when she supped with him on 14 July 1677, were La Rochefoucauld, M. and Mme de Coulanges, M. le Duc (as Condé's eldest son, the Duc de Bourbon, was always called), M. de Barillon (on a holiday from England), M. de Briole, Charles de Sévigné, Mme de Frontenac, and Mme de Schomberg, the second wife of the well-known Maréchal de Schomberg, who was killed at the battle of the Boyne. Judging from Mme de Sévigné's report of an interview that she had with Louis XIV, she had a pretty wit and was quite capable of holding her own in the thrust and parry of conversation.[2] Mme de La Fayette struck up a great friendship with her—a friendship which from its suddenness caused Mme de Sévigné some amusement, and perhaps a little jealousy.[3]

[1] *Mémoires de Gourville*, ed. L. Lecestre, 2 vols. 1894. He no doubt exaggerates the importance of the various parts that he played. See Saint-Simon, *Mémoires*, III, 421–423 (an excellent notice).

[2] 30 July 1677.

[3] 30 October and 1 November 1680.

M. le Duc "more like a gnome than a man" (Mme de Caylus) and who according to his son-in-law, Lassay, "had not a single virtue" and "would have been the most malignant man on earth, if he had not been the feeblest", was remarkably intelligent and well-informed and could be most agreeable when it suited him. The Comte de Briole, or Briord, was his master of the horse (*premier écuyer*), and afterwards became ambassador first at Turin and then at The Hague. The rest of the party we know already. It was given in a pavilion of the Hôtel de Condé, which Gourville had recently built.[1] There was a garden with fountains and alleys, in which oboes, flutes, violins and a *basse de viole* (the earlier form of the violoncello) played in the moonlight. "Un souper enchanté."[2]

On an earlier occasion, in December 1673, the guests besides Mme de Sévigné were La Rochefoucauld and his son, M. de Marsillac, Mme de La Fayette, M. le Duc, Mme de Coulanges, Mme de Thianges, Mme de Montespan's sister, who had a fair share of the Mortemart wit, M. de Guilleragues, and the Abbé Têtu. The Comte de Guilleragues, Secretary to the Cabinet, to whom Boileau dedicated his Fifth Epistle, was the translator of the famous *Lettres Portugaises* (1669)[3] of the Portuguese nun, Marianna Alcaforada. According to Saint-Simon he was greedy, amusing, witty, and an incurable spendthrift. It was he, according

---

[1] The site of the Hôtel de Condé is now occupied by the Odéon and the adjoining streets, of which one is the Rue de Condé.

[2] 16 July 1677.

[3] Ed. Asse, 1873, and see above, p. 61.

to Mme de Sévigné, who said that Pellisson, the historian of the Académie Française, had abused a man's privilege of being ugly. He had been an admirer of Mme de Maintenon in the days when she was Mme Scarron, and Saint-Simon says that it was due to her that he was appointed ambassador to Constantinople, where he died.[1]

The conversation at these parties, where most of the guests were more or less on intimate terms with one another, must have been delightful—easy, witty, and well-bred. We may suppose that they observed La Rochefoucauld's admirable maxims on the subject, especially, let us hope, the most important of all—"S'il y a beaucoup d'art à savoir parler à propos, il n'y en a moins à savoir se taire."

In a letter written on Ash Wednesday (23 February) 1689, Mme de Sévigné mentions supper-parties on the three preceding evenings. On Sunday the host was Jean de Camus, Civil Lieutenant of the Châtelet, who had a high reputation for learning and probity. The other guests were Mme du Lude, Mme de Coulanges, the Chevalier de Grignan, Corbinelli, Mme de Saint-Germain, and the Bishop of Troyes, "Nous fûmes assez gaillards".[2] On Monday she supped "en toute familiarité" with M. de Lamoignon, the only other guests being Coulanges and the Abbé Bigorre, and on Shrove Tuesday with Mme de Coulanges, the other guests being Mme de Chaulnes and *les Divines*. Sometimes she herself is the hostess as, for instance, when on the eve of her departure for Vichy in May 1676

[1] *Mémoires*, I, 347.   [2] 21 February 1689.

M. and Mme de Coulanges, M. de La Trousse, Mme de La Troche, Corbinelli, and Mlle de Montgeron, came to say farewell and eat a pigeon-pie.[1]

If Mme de Sévigné's affection for her friends was warm and constant, they responded to it with a loyal and admiring devotion. Whenever she returned after a considerable absence they hastened to greet her. On the very day that she reached Paris in November 1673, after a four weeks' journey from Provence, a crowd of visitors came to Coulanges's house in the Rue du Parc-Royal to welcome her back and hear her account of her daughter's new home. She was very tired and her nose was red with the wind, but she determined to see her friends. Nearly all of them we know already. Only three have not yet been mentioned—Mme de Sanzei, an aunt of Mme de Sévigné, Mme de Bagnols, who was Mme de Coulanges's sister-in-law, and the Archbishop of Reims, a brother of Louvois, whose name often appears in Mme de Sévigné's letters. Among them was Mme Scarron, still living in the Rue de Vaugirard. On the next morning at 9 o'clock, the Chevalier de Grignan, La Garde, Brancas, and d'Hacqueville came up to her room "pour raisonner ce qu'on appelle raisonner pantoufle", that is to say, to chatter about this, that, and the other.[2]

But more instructive are the names of the friends who came to say good-bye to her when she left Paris in the middle of April 1689, just after Easter, for her long residence at Les Rochers.[3] I give them in the same order that she does—Mme du Lude and her mother,

[1] 10 May 1676.   [2] 2 November 1673.   [3] 2 May 1689.

Mme de Verneuil, Mme de Coulanges—all these from the convents, where they were presumably making a retreat—Mme de Vins, Mme d'Huxelles, Mme de Mouci, Mlle de La Rochefoucauld, and (the only man among them), M. Du Bois. She had embraced Mme de La Fayette the evening before and Mme de Chaulnes was her travelling companion. All these women, except Mme de Vins and Mme du Lude, were among Mme de Sévigné's oldest friends. Of her men friends, Retz, La Rochefoucauld, Brancas, d'Hacqueville, Guitaut, and *le bien Bon* were dead. Coulanges was staying with Lamoignon at Basville; the Duc de Chaulnes was at Rennes; Barillon was in England, fulfilling his duties as ambassador; the Président de Moulceau was at Montpellier; Pomponne and La Garde were probably at their country seats; and so certainly was Bussy, for Mme de Sévigné had recently written to him there. The Chevalier de Grignan had gone to drink the waters at Balarue-les-Bains, not far from Montpellier; Corbinelli had only just left the Hôtel de Carnavalet, where he had been living; and Mlle de Méri, who was certainly living there in the previous year, may have been there still, or she may have been indisposed. I miss also Mme de La Troche. With her addition we have, I think, all Mme de Sévigné's intimate friends.

One is struck both by their distinction and by their high characters. More than two-thirds figure in Saint-Simon's pages, and of at least ten of these he speaks in terms of the highest praise. The only two of whom he says anything—and that not much—by way of dispraise are Mme d'Huxelles and Mme de Mouci, and we have seen that he was prejudiced against both. But from Mme de Sévigné's letters alone, without any testimony from other sources, we get a remarkable impression of the high quality of her intimate friends. Among the men were diplomatists, magistrates, and other public officials; men who were either men of letters themselves or were in close touch with the literary world; and men distinguished in society as wits or conversationalists. The only distinguished soldier is the Duc du Lude, and though Mme de Sévigné was on friendly terms with several bishops, and with other distinguished ecclesiastics, like Bourdaloue and Mascaron, with none of them does she seem to have been really intimate. Among the women were popular hostesses, like Mme d'Huxelles and Mme de Coulanges, and women of great beauty like Mme de Vins, Mme de Verneuil and her daughter, Mme du Lude, not to speak of Mme de Coulanges.

They are, on the whole, as remarkable for character as for ability. Arnauld d'Andilly and his son Pomponne, the Duc and Duchesse de Chaulnes, La Garde, Têtu, Corbinelli, Mme du Lude, Mme de Vins, the saintly Mme de Mouci were all of the highest character. Mme de Lavardin had her defects; she was fond of money and her own comforts, but she had a "bon et solide esprit". Mme de La Troche was quick to take offence and given to jealousy, but she was extraordinarily kind and helpful, hardly less so than d'Hacqueville, who was never weary of doing services for his friends. M. and Mme de Guitaut were an excellent and intelligent couple, the husband more lively and amusing, the wife more serious. We know M. de Moulceau only from Mme de Sévigné's and Corbinelli's letters to him, but evidently he was a man of high character and intelligence, well worthy of their friendship.

I pointed out that all the friends who came to say farewell to Mme de Sévigné before she went to Les Rochers for what proved to be her last visit there were with two exceptions, Mme de Vins and Mme du Lude, very old friends, friends of forty years or more. She had known Mme de Vins for over fifteen years, and though she does not seem to have seen much of Mme du Lude before her marriage to the Duke in 1681, she doubtless knew her as a girl, being, as she was, on very friendly terms with her mother the Duchesse de Verneuil. It is the same with her men friends; only the Chevalier de Grignan, La Garde, and M. de Moulceau were friends that she made after her daughter's marriage and they were all the result of that marriage, for the first two were relations of her son-in-law, and M. de Moulceau she met at Montpellier when she paid a short visit there from Grignan.

I have included among the intimate friends of Mme de Sévigné all of those with whom she had frequent relations or with whom it appears from her letters that she was on familiar terms. Perhaps I have used the word "intimate" in too wide a sense. But even if you confine it to the meaning of friends on whom you could rely in time of trouble, which is after all the ultimate test of friendship, one can, I think, find at least a dozen, or perhaps more, of Mme de Sévigné's friends who can be termed intimate in its more exclusive sense. And the experience of most persons will surely be that this is a large number. Most persons, too, will testify that their own experience is much the same as Mme de Sévigné's, namely, that after the age of forty or forty-five one makes few great friends, except in special circumstances.

The devotion to Mme de Sévigné of her old friends was equalled by her devotion to them. Her letters to Coulanges, when he was at Rome with the Duc de Chaulnes in 1690, and even more those that she wrote to him from Grignan during the last year of her life, are full of a cousinly affection which time could not diminish. The letters to Rome contain many affectionate and appreciative references to her "cher Ambassadeur", and in one of them she speaks of her great sorrow for the dangerous illness of "her old and intimate friend", Mme de Lavardin, "cette illustre veuve, qui nous avoit toutes rassemblées sous son aile". She had heard the news—she was writing from Grignan—from Mme de Chaulnes, who was greatly grieved. Mme de La Fayette felt it even more.[1] Mme de Lavardin lingered on, as we have seen, for three years, and in the pathetic little letter of 24 January 1692, Mme de La Fayette complains that owing to the horrible cold she cannot go and see her. She herself was very ill at the time and she died in the night of 25–26 May 1693. I have already quoted the passage of her letter in which she tells Mme de Sévigné that she is the person in the world whom she has loved best, and also the passage from Mme de Sévigné's letter

[1] 10 April 1691.

to Mme de Guitaut after Mme de La Fayette's death, in which she says that there had never been the least cloud in their friendship.[1] What better testimony can we have to the friendship between two of the greatest Frenchwomen of the seventeenth century?

Of the deep affection which united Mme de Sévigné to what we may call the inner circle of her friends there is no doubt. We have seen how warmly they welcomed her on her return after a few months' absence and how tenderly they bid her farewell when she set out on a fresh departure. In the next chapter we shall see how perturbed they were when from motives of economy she proposed to stay at Les Rochers throughout the winter, and how the Duchesse de Chaulnes and other friends tried to make an arrangement which would enable her to spend the winter with her friends in Paris without too great expense. The Coulanges were, we know, always ready to receive her in their *hôtel*, when she was temporarily homeless, and she in her turn, when Mme de Coulanges was seriously ill, was constantly at her bedside.

[1] See above, p. 29.

III

MME DE SÉVIGNÉ AT LIVRY & LES ROCHERS

Besides the Mme de Sévigné of Paris and society, who collected the latest news of the army and the Court for her daughter's benefit, there was also a Mme de Sévigné who loved nature and solitude and meditation. These she found at Livry and Les Rochers. At Livry *le bien Bon* had built for her a pavilion in the precincts of his abbey, and here from time to time she would betake herself, either alone or with one or two friends, whenever she felt that "the world was too much with her". Situated at the edge of the forest of Bondy it is about eleven miles from the centre of Paris. Horace Walpole made a pilgrimage there in 1766 and describes it in a letter to his friend, George Montagu:

The Abbé's house is decent and snug; a few paces from it is the sacred pavilion built for Madame de Sévigné by her uncle, and much as it was in her day; a small saloon below for dinner, then an arcade, but the niches now closed, and painted in fresco with medallions of her, the Grignan, the Fayette, and the Rochefoucauld. Above, a handsome large room, with a chimney-piece in the best taste of Louis the Fourteenth's time; a holy family in good relief over it, and the cypher of her uncle Coulanges; a neat little bedchamber within, and two or three clean little chambers over them. On one side of the garden, leading to the great road, is a little bridge of wood, on which the dear woman used to wait for the courier that brought her daughter's letters.[1]

Horace Walpole's last sentence is pathetically illustrated by the first letter that the "dear woman" wrote from Livry after the separation from her daughter. It was written on the Tuesday before Easter (24 March 1671). Every line is full of pathos, and I must quote the greater part of it:

Il y a trois heures que je suis ici, ma chère enfant. Je suis partie de Paris avec l'Abbé, Hélène, Hébert et Marphise, dans le dessein de me retirer ici du monde et du bruit jusqu'à jeudi au soir. Je prétends être en solitude; je fais de ceci une petite Trappe; je veux y prier Dieu, y faire mille réflexions. J'ai dessein d'y jeûner beaucoup par toutes sortes de raisons; marcher pour tout le temps que j'ai été dans ma chambre, et sur le tout m'ennuyer pour l'amour de Dieu. Mais, ma pauvre bonne, ce que je ferai beaucoup mieux que tout cela, c'est de penser à vous. Je n'ai pas encore cessé depuis que je suis arrivée, et ne pouvant contenir tous mes sentiments sur votre sujet, je me suis mené à vous écrire au bout de cette petite allée sombre que vous aimez, assise sur ce siège de mousse où je vous ai vue quelquefois couchée. Mais, mon Dieu! où ne vous ai-je point vue ici? et de quelle façon toutes ces pensées me traversent-elles le cœur? Il n'y a point d'endroit, point de lieu, ni dans la maison, ni dans l'église, ni dans ce pays, ni dans ce jardin, où je ne vous aie vue; il n'y en a point qui ne me fasse souvenir de quelque chose; et de quelque façon que ce soit aussi, cela me perce le cœur.

[1] This is quoted by Mrs Aldis in her *The Queen of Letter-writers*, 1907, pp. 15–17. She describes the present condition of the place; the pavilion has been pulled down.

Two days later she writes:

J'ai trouvé de la douceur dans la tristesse que j'ai eue ici; une grande solitude, un grand silence, un office triste des ténèbres chantées avec dévotion (je n'avois jamais été à Livry la semaine sainte), un jeûne canonique, et une beauté dans ces jardins dont vous seriez charmée: tout cela m'a plu.

She adds that she is returning to Paris partly in order to hear the Good Friday sermon of either Bourdaloue or Mascaron: "J'ai toujours honoré les belles Passions." At all seasons of the year she found Livry beautiful. "J'arrivai hier au soir ici, ma très-chère", she writes in July 1677; "il y fait parfaitement beau; j'y suis seule, et dans une paix, un silence, un loisir dont je suis ravie." She stayed ten days there on this occasion and was joined by her son, with whom she read *Don Quixote*, Lucian, and the *Lettres Provinciales*. A letter of August 1675 expresses in a few words the sense of repose and peace that she found there: "Je suis venue ce matin toute seule, fatiguée et lassée de Paris au point de n'y pouvoir pas durer.... Me voilà donc pour trois jours en paix et en repos." In the following year (1676), the year in which she drank the waters at Vichy, after her attack of rheumatic fever, she spent a considerable time at Livry—about half of the three months from 12 August to 13 November.

A specially interesting letter from Livry is one written on Ash Wednesday (6 March) 1680. She had gone there with a few friends on the previous Saturday and the brilliance of the sunshine had tempted them to prolong their stay:

Nous avons tempéré le brillant de carême...prenant avec la feuille morte de cette forêt; il y a fait le plus beau temps du monde; les jardins sont propres, la vue belle, et un bruit des oiseaux qui commencent déjà d'annoncer le printemps, qui nous a paru bien plus joli que les vilains cris des rues de Paris.

The party consisted of *le bien Bon*, the Bishop of Rennes, the Abbé du Pile, and Coulanges. They walked and talked, and played at chess and backgammon, and sometimes at cards; they read plays, and the *Lettres Provinciales*, and *La Princesse de Clèves*, which *ces prêtres* enthusiastically admired. When Mme de Sévigné returned to Paris on the evening of Ash Wednesday, she found La Rochefoucauld seriously ill. He died a fortnight later, on the 17th of March.

Les Rochers in Brittany, three miles from Vitré, which Mme de Sévigné inherited from her husband, is, unlike Livry, in more or less the same condition as she left it. The house is of the fifteenth century, with steep slated roofs, especially those of the three turrets. The circular chapel, which the Abbé built, is a separate building, and looks rather like a massive dovecot.[1] In front of the château is a large square, called *La Place Madame*, and behind it a formal garden, laid out by Mme de Sévigné with the help of plans and drawings by Le Nôtre, whom she had probably known in the days when he designed the great gardens of Vaux-le-Vicomte for Foucquet. Whether after the fashion of the day there was an orangery, is not clear, but at any rate

[1] See J. Aldis, *op. cit.* p. 222 for an illustration. I only know it from this, but I see that Boissier in his *Mme de Sévigné* (*Les grands Écrivains français*) finds the same resemblance to a dovecot.

there were orange-trees in tubs, and Mme de Sévigné loved the scent of their blossom. There was also a sun-dial with the inscription, *Ultimam time*.

The park was separated from the garden by an iron railing and an open space called *La Place de Coulanges*. When Mme de Sévigné became *châtelaine*, there were no doubt many trees, either dotted about or in groups, but with the love of formality which characterised the classical age she set to work to introduce order and symmetry. She cut down trees and planted others so as to form *allées* or walks, which were doubtless gravelled. Many of them bore names such as *L'Infini* and *Le Solitaire*. Of the latter, which she made in the autumn of 1680, she was very proud. At one end of it was a labyrinth and at the other a large open space surrounded by four rows of trees and called the cloister. Here was the termination of the broad alley or *mail*, where Mme de Sévigné's guests sometimes played the game of that name.[1] One of her chief pleasures was in watching her woodcutters at work. This she graphically describes in a letter of 20 November 1675:

Je m'amuse à faire abattre de grands arbres; le tracas que cela fait représente au naturel ces tapisseries, où l'on peint les ouvrages de l'hyver; des arbres qu'on abat, des gens qui scient, d'autres qui font des bûches, d'autres qui chargent une charette, et moi, au milieu, voilà le tableau. Je m'en vais planter: *car* que faire aux Rochers, à moins que l'on ne plante.

During her last sojourn at Les Rochers in 1689 and 1690, we hear of no more planting. Not, I feel sure,

[1] See letters of 8 September 1680 and 12 January 1676.

because at sixty-three she felt too old to plant; for she would have quoted her favourite La Fontaine's fable, *Un octogénaire plantoit*, but, as she was then economising in every direction, she would have regarded planting and making walks as an unnecessary expense.

During the period of her correspondence with her daughter, Mme de Sévigné paid five visits to Les Rochers, at intervals of about four and a half years, the first being made not long after the first separation from her daughter. She set out from Paris on Monday, 18 May 1671, accompanied by *le bien Bon*, the Abbé La Mousse, her son Charles, her *valet-de-chambre* Hébert, her maid Hélène, and her dog Marphise. Madame and *le bien Bon* travelled in a caleche and pair, the others in another caleche with four horses and a postilion. There were three or four men on horseback, of whom, no doubt, the valet was one, and there was a pack-horse, which carried Mme de Sévigné's bed. Sometimes *le bien Bon* changed places with Charles, and then the two Abbés read their breviary together, while Mme de Sévigné and Charles read "a certain breviary of Corneille". On Saturday the 23rd they reached Malicorne, about 130 miles from Paris, and about ten miles beyond Le Mans, where M. de Lavardin, the son of Mme de Sévigné's great friend, had a château. Here they spent a night and, making an early start at 2 a.m. the next morning on account of the heat, they arrived at Les Rochers, a distance of about fifty-six miles, on Wednesday the 27th.[1]

On the next occasion Mme de Sévigné travelled part

[1] 13 and 23 May 1671.

of the way by water. Having driven to Orleans she transferred herself and her carriage to a hired *cabane*, as the boats on the Loire were called. Leaving Orleans on 11 September 1675, she stopped at Veret, Tours, Saumur and Ingrandes and arrived at Nantes on 20 September. She had expected to arrive on the 17th, but the boat ran aground close to Nantes. She stayed a week at Nantes and after spending two nights at La Silleraye, with M. d'Harrouys, she reached Les Rochers on the 26th.[1] The grounding of the boat was not a very unusual event, for the Loire has always been subject to extremes of high and low water. But in the sixteenth and seventeenth centuries it was much used for the transport of travellers and materials. La Fontaine in 1663 compares the river at Orleans to a miniature Bosphorus, and John Evelyn in 1644 went by boat most of the way from Orleans to Amboise. The rate of progress, of course, depended upon the wind, but the stopping-places mentioned by Mme de Sévigné shew that the average run was about forty-five miles for a day of twelve to fourteen hours.

It will be noticed that Mme de Sévigné did not leave Paris in this year till the middle of September. Her daughter had been with her till nearly the end of May, but she prolonged her stay owing to the disturbed state of Brittany. In 1680 she again travelled by boat, stopping at Blois instead of at Veret and arriving at Nantes on 13 May, four days after leaving Orleans. On this occasion there was no running aground. She had *le bien Bon* with her and they sat comfortably in her

[1] 11, 14, 17, 20, 24 and 26 September 1675.

carriage, which was so arranged on the boat that they were not inconvenienced by the sun and had a beautiful view before them. From Blois she writes that she has heard a thousand nightingales and from Tours and again from Ingrandes that she has never seen such lovely scenery.[1]

In November 1680 Mme de Grignan joined her mother in Paris, and the two were together till September 1684, when Mme de Sévigné went to Les Rochers on business and stayed there till the following August. Again she took boat at Orleans, but this time she slept the first night at Saint-Dié, not having been able to get as far as Blois. The second night was spent at Amboise. It does not appear where she stopped between Amboise and Saumur, but it was not at Tours. At Les Ponts de Cé she left the boat for Angers and went by road from there to Les Rochers.[2]

Mme de Sévigné's descriptions of her Breton neighbours and of Breton life are well known. The genial Duc de Chaulnes, the Governor of the province, and his warm-hearted wife; the Protestant Princesse de Tarente, aunt to the second Madame; M. d'Harrouys, "cet esprit supérieur à toutes les choses qui font les occupations des autres, cette âme aussi grande que celle de M. Turenne"; that amusing original, the Marquis de Pomenars, who always had a criminal prosecution hanging over his head and was in fact prosecuted for coining false money, and who just before a severe operation made his confession—the first for four years

---

[1] 8, 9, 11 and 12 May 1680.
[2] 16, 18 and 20 September 1684.

—to Bourdaloue—"une belle confession", which lasted four hours; and Mlle Du Plessis d'Argentré, a near neighbour, whose affectations and oddities were an unfailing source of amusement to Mme de Sévigné and her daughter—these are all familiar figures. We know too her humbler neighbours, gypsies and peasants, in particular the man who arrived laden with sacks of money, some under his arms, some in his pockets, some in his trousers, and who when *le bien Bon*, "thinking that our fortunes were made", asked him how much he had brought, replied "thirty francs", the whole sum being in *doubles* or double *deniers*, so that as a *double* is worth only the sixth of a *sou*, there must have been 3600 pieces. All these characters Mme de Sévigné portrays for us in varying degrees of distinctiveness, and it will be observed that in so doing she employs most of the methods of a skilful novelist or dramatist. In one person she notes some peculiar physical feature, in another a mental trait; some develop gradually, as they pass across the stage; some present themselves by characteristic speech. With nearly all she is in friendly sympathy, and if there is satire, there is never malice. There is no effort, no deliberate attempt to draw a portrait; she is a spontaneous creator if ever there was one. For her men and women are just as truly creations as the imaginary beings of a novelist or a dramatist. They live only in her letters.

But I am now concerned with Mme de Sévigné, not in relation with others, but in solitude and repose, in communio n with her own soul. In her first summer at Les Rochers after the separation from her daughter she writes that the Abbé La Mousse being indisposed with a tooth-ache and *le bien Bon* with a bad knee, she can walk in her mall as she pleases.

Il me plaît de m'y promener le soir jusqu'à huit heures; mon fils n'y est plus; cela fait un silence, une tranquillité et une solitude que je ne crois pas qu'il soit aisé de rencontrer ailleurs. Je ne vous dis point à qui je pense, ni avec quelque tendresse; quand on devine, il n'est pas besoin de parler.

And she quotes the first stanza of Saint-Amant's ode to Solitude.[1]

It is in the letters written during her second visit that we find the most frequent expressions of delight in the beauty of her words. In her first letter after her arrival in September she writes:

J'ai trouvé ces bois d'une beauté et d'une tristesse extraordinaire; tous les arbres que vous avez vus petits sont devenus grands et droits, et beaux en perfection: ils sont élagués, et font une ombre agréable; ils ont quarante et cinquante pieds de hauteur: il y a un petit air d'amour maternel dans ce détail; songez que je les ai tous plantés, et que je les ai vus, comme disoit M. de Montbason, *pas plus grands que cela*. C'est ici une solitude faite exprès pour y bien rêver.[2]

And a month later she writes:

Ces bois sont toujours beaux: le verd en est cent fois plus beau que celui de Livry. Je ne sais si c'est la qualité des arbres ou la fraîcheur des pluies; mais il n'y a pas de comparaison; tout y est encore aujourd'hui du même verd du mois de Mai: les feuilles qui tombent sont feuille-morte; mais celles qui tienne encore sont vertes: vous n'avez jamais observé cette beauté.[3]

[1] II, 279.   [2] 29 September 1675.   [3] 20 October 1675.

Mme de Sévigné's love of nature was perfectly genuine; her descriptions are the result of personal observation and not of literary reminiscence. But it would be a mistake to suppose that she was a close observer of nature. She noted the passage of the seasons; she took pleasure in the changing colour of the leaves and in the varying effects of dawn and mid-day and twilight; and she welcomed the first song of mating birds. But, so far as we can judge from her letters, her interest and her knowledge were merely of a general character. She mentions no flowers by name, except orange blossom, nor any trees except the oaks and beeches that she happened to be planting. She writes from Livry that "the nightingale, the cuckoo and the *fauvette* (probably the blackcap) have opened the spring", and she laughs at her daughter for saying that she had heard a nightingale sing at the end of June. When she laments over the trees that her son had cut down at Buron she speaks of the vanished *corbeaux* and *chouettes*, probably, rooks and brown owls.[1] But evidently her knowledge either of trees or animals does not go far.

Nevertheless, she is rightly regarded as one of the few writers of the age of Louis XIV who loved nature. Her attitude greatly resembles Bossuet's. He too loved the spring, when the green leaves opened on the trees and the flowers carpeted the fields and woods. His description of a sunrise from a personal experience is famous. He loved, too, his garden at Meaux. Like

[1] *Corbeau* is properly a raven, and *chouette* a short-eared owl, but both words are used loosely.

Mme de Sévigné's, it was formerly planned with two broad intersecting gravelled walks, and it had a labyrinth and an orangery.[1] In *Les Amours de Psyché* La Fontaine says that Acaste "aimait extrêmement les jardins, les fleurs, les ombrages", and that he recited a charming poem of his own composition, which has the following verse:

> Orangers, arbres que j'adore
> Que vos parfums me semblent doux !
> Est-il dans l'empire de Flore
> Rien d'agréable comme vous?

In this winter Mme de Sévigné at the age of fifty had her first real illness. It was a sharp attack of rheumatism; it began with a ricked neck (*torticolis*) and severe pain in her right side, which prevented her sleeping or even resting comfortably. Her legs, feet, arms, and hands were much swollen, especially her hands, so that Charles either wrote to Mme de Grignan for her, or else wrote at her dictation. There was a good doctor at Vitré, M. de l'Orme, who bled her, as was usual, on the foot and gave her a powder which worked wonders. At the end of a fortnight she was free from pain and fever and a week later she dictated to Charles a letter, which begins with a graphic account of her experience:

Devinez ce que c'est, mon enfant, que la chose du monde, qui vient le plus vite, et qui s'en va le plus lentement, qui vous fait approcher le plus près de la

---

[1] See "Dans les Jardins de M. de Meaux ou Bossuet et la nature", a chapter in M. Philippe Bertault's charming *Bossuet intime*, 1927. See especially p. 41 for a description of the garden, and p. 80 for a photograph of it.

convalescence, et qui vous en retire le plus loin, qui vous fait toucher l'état du monde le plus agréable, et qui vous empêche le plus d'en jouir, qui vous donne les plus belles espérances, et qui en éloigne le plus l'effet: ne sauriez vous le deviner? *jetez-vous votre langue aux chiens?*[1] c'est le rhumatisme.[2]

Her hands were still swollen when she left Les Rochers on 24 March; so to complete her recovery she went to Vichy on 10 May, and after her cure, which lasted a month, she could report that her hands were no longer swollen, though she could not close them. The rheumatism left no ill-effects and ten years later she could speak of her "belle et triomphante santé".[3]

On 14 April 1689 Mme de Sévigné left Paris for what proved to be her last visit to Les Rochers. She had sold her horses and was therefore glad to accept Mme de Chaulnes's offer of a seat in her carriage. They spent ten days at Chaulnes, which is about equidistant from Amiens and Saint-Quentin, and then went by Rouen, Caen, Avranches, Dol to Rennes. Here a fortnight later Mme de Sévigné was joined by Charles and his wife, and the three left on 25 May to reach Les Rochers the same evening. "J'ai un véritable besoin de me reposer", writes Mme de Sévigné, "et de me taire dans ces aimables bois." Her visit on this occasion was largely dictated by a desire to economise. The large fortune which she possessed at the time of her marriage was greatly reduced by her debauched

---

[1] Do you give it up?
[2] 3 February 1676, and see letters from 12 January to 24 March.
[3] 3 April 1686 (to M. de Moulceau).

and spendthrift husband. In spite of the good management and economy of her uncle and her own good sense and instinct for affairs, the transference to her son and daughter of their shares in the property left her with a greatly diminished income, out of which she often came to their assistance. Charles, though a much better fellow than his father, threatened to tread in his footsteps. He was at any rate a spendthrift, and his mother's account of him could not be bettered as a description of spendthrifts in general:

Il trouve l'intention de dépenser sans paroître, de perdre sans jouer, et de payer sans s'acquitter; toujours une soif et un besoin d'argent, en paix comme en guerre; c'est un abîme de je ne sais quoi, car il n'a aucune fantaisie, mais sa main est un creuset qui fond l'argent.

But he was more weak than wicked, and in 1684, having become a reformed character, he married a Mlle Mauron, the daughter of a Councillor of the Rennes *Parlement*, who had a considerable fortune. On the other hand the Grignan family continued to be a constant source of financial anxiety to Mme de Sévigné and it was on their account that she retired to Les Rochers and practised the utmost economy.

The difficulties of M. and Mme de Grignan had arisen in this way. As one of the King's Lieutenant-Generals for Languedoc and as acting governor of Provence, M. de Grignan had embarked on a career of extravagant display such as his royal master loved and encouraged. Moreover, both he and his wife were naturally extravagant and were gamblers into the bargain. The result was that they spent far beyond their income, and in 1689 their fortunes were in an almost desperate condition. Thus Mme de Sévigné, when she came to Les Rochers in the summer of this year, had before her the double task of practising strict economy and of managing her estate so as to get as much out of it as possible. The combination of high courage and sound business capacity that she shewed at this crisis is worthy of all praise.

Unfortunately *le bien Bon*, who ever since her husband's death had devoted himself to her interests and had taken so large a part in the management of her property, was no longer with her. He had died in April 1687 at the age of eighty-four. Seven months later, in a letter to Bussy, of 13 November, she refers to him in a passage which I cannot resist transcribing, for it not only expresses in beautiful language her gratitude to her uncle, but it records with perfect simplicity the salient features of her own character:

Je lui devois la douceur et le repos de ma vie; c'est à lui à qui vous devez la joie que j'apportois dans votre société; sans lui, nous n'aurions jamais si ensemble: vous lui devez toute ma gayeté, ma belle humeur, ma vivacité, le don que j'avois de vous bien entendre, l'intelligence qui me faisoit comprendre ce que vous aviez dit, et deviner ce que vous alliez dire; en un mot, le bon Abbé en me retirant des abymes où M. de Sévigné m'avoit laissée, m'a rendue telle que j'étois, telle que vous m'avez vue, et digne de votre estime, et de votre amitié. Je tire le rideau sur vos torts; ils sont grands, mais il les faut oublier, et vous dire que j'ai senti vivement la perte de cette agréable source de tout le repos de ma vie.[1]

[1] 13 November 1687.

Ma gayeté, ma belle humeur, ma vivacité. What could be truer? And the reader will take note of the last sentence, and, remembering Bussy's atrocious slanders in *L'Histoire amoureuse des Gaules*, will also recognise the large and forgiving nature of the writer.

Two letters, written one near the end of June, the other in the middle of September, show us how she ordinarily spent her day.[1] There is very little difference between the two accounts, except that in summer she naturally passed more of her time in the open air. At first she did not greatly take to her daughter-in-law, who was delicate and complaining and without much resource. However, she gradually got to like her better and found her not only full of good sense herself but able to impart it to her husband. In 1689 they were a devoted couple, Charles with "un fonds de philosophie chrétienne, chamarrée d'un brin d'anachorète". He was a delightful companion, a lover of good literature, and a tender and affectionate son. When, however, the first letter was written, he was temporarily absent.

But to come to Mme de Sévigné's day. She got up at eight and, after a walk in the wood in summer, went to Mass at nine. Then she completed her toilette, said good morning, walked, if it was fine, and picked orange blossoms. After dinner, which was doubtless at twelve, they read and worked till five. When Charles was not there, Mme de Sévigné was the reader, that she might spare her daughter-in-law, whose chest was weak. At five they separated, and in summer Mme de

[1] 29 June and 18 September 1689.

Sévigné went out alone to read and meditate until the bell rang for supper at eight—"entre chien et loup":[1]

Je m'en vais dans ces aimables allées; j'ai un laquais qui me suit, j'ai des livres, je change de place, et je varie le tour de mes promenades: un livre de dévotion et un livre d'histoire: on va de l'un à l'autre, cela fait du divertissement; on peut rêver à Dieu, à sa Providence, posséder son âme, songer à l'avenir.

In the shorter days of September there was naturally less walking and more reading between five o'clock and supper. Charles, who read admirably and could read aloud for five hours at a stretch, was the reader, and, as in June, the book was either a historical or a devotional work. In earlier days it had often been Molière, and sometimes Rabelais. Afterwards they discussed what they had read. A good deal of time, especially by Mme de Sévigné, was spent in letter-writing. After supper Charles read to them again, "lively books for fear of going to sleep". At ten the young couple retired, but Mme de Sévigné did not go to bed till nearly midnight: "Voilà quelle est à peu près le règle de notre couvent: il y a sur la porte, *sainte liberté*, ou *fais ce que tu voudras*."

In the short passage that I have quoted from the June letter Mme de Sévigné says that during her morning promenade she can "meditate on God and His Providence, and possess her soul". She was no mystic, and she was not *dévote* though, as she says in one of her letters, to be *dévote* was one of her greatest

[1] I.e. the time when you cannot distinguish a dog from a wolf. Mme de Sévigné writes "pendant l'entre-chien et loup".

94

wishes. She was an ordinary Christian, keeping to the
faith in which she had been brought up, fasting in
Lent and on Fridays and communicating regularly but
not frequently. In a letter written in January 1690 she
explains her religion very clearly to her daughter:

Vous me demandez si je suis toujours une petite
dévote qui ne vant guère; oui justement, voilà ce que
je suis toujours, et pas davantage à mon grand regret.
Tout ce que j'ai de bon, c'est que je sais bien ma
religion, et de quoi il est question: je ne prendrai
point le faux pour le vrai; je démêle ce qui est solide
de ce qui n'en a que l'apparence; j'espère ne point m'y
méprendre, et que Dieu m'ayant déjà donné de bons
sentiments, m'en donnera encore: les graces passées me
garantissent en quelque sorte celles qui viendront; en
sorte que je vis à la confiance, mêlées pourtant de
beaucoup de craintes.[1]

In the same letter she defends her friend Corbinelli, who
had recently proclaimed himself a mystic, against her
daughter's sarcasm. "I uphold", she says, "the faithful admirer of St Theresa, of my grandmother, and of
the blessed John of the Cross."[2] Mme de Sévigné was
fifteen when her grandmother, Sainte Chantal, died and
she always had for her the greatest admiration and
reverence. From her, no doubt, she learnt to pay a
similar regard to the Mère Angélique of Port-Royal,
the friend of Sainte Chantal during the last twenty
years of the latter's life. Then through her husband's
uncle, Renaud de Sévigné, who went to live at Port-

[1] 15 January 1690.
[2] Sainte Chantal was canonised in 1767, and St John of the
Cross in 1726.

Royal in 1656, she came to know several of his Port-Royal friends, especially the members of the great Arnauld clan. The Abbé Antoine Arnauld, author of memoirs, the eldest son of Arnauld d'Andilly, says that he was introduced to her in 1657, and her earliest letter to his brother Pomponne was written in 1661, the year in which Mère Angélique died. With him and with his father Arnauld d'Andilly, whom she always calls *le bon homme*, she was, as we have seen, on terms of close affection, and she knew well another brother Henri, the saintly bishop of Angers. Of their sister, the younger Mère Angélique, who became Abbess of Port-Royal in 1678, she speaks with the warmest admiration: "C'est la première fois que j'ai vu une religieuse parler et penser en religieuse", and of Port-Royal itself, after a brief visit to her uncle, Renaud de Sévigné, she writes with eloquent enthusiasm:

Ce Port-Royal est une Thébaïde; c'est un Paradis; c'est un désert où toute la dévotion du christianisme s'est rangée; c'est une sainteté répandue dans tout le pays à une lieue à la ronde.

She not only admired the Port-Royalists, but she delighted in their literature: "Personne n'a encore écrit comme ces Messieurs; car je mets Pascal de moitié à tout ce qui est beau." We know what she thought of *Les Provinciales*—*les petites lettres*, as she always calls them—and she found Nicole's *Essais de Morale* "delicious". She does not seem to have been personally acquainted with *le grand* Arnauld, who was the youngest brother of *le bon homme*, but she was seventeen when his widely read book, *La Fréquente Communion*, appeared (1643), and she came to know it well. She used as books of devotion Saint-Cyran's *Letters, Un Traité de la Prière perpétuelle* by the saintly physician of Port-Royal, Jean Hamon, published apparently soon after his death in 1687,[1] and *L'Année chrétienne* by Nicolas Le Tourneux, the confessor of Port-Royal.

If Mme de Sévigné's devotional reading was chiefly in Jansenist works, her favourite preacher was a Jesuit —Bourdaloue. When he first preached at Paris, his fame had already preceded him and his Advent course for 1669 at the Jesuit house in the Rue Saint-Antoine attracted large crowds. In the following year he preached during Advent before the Court at the Tuileries, and Mme de Sévigné reports that he "preached divinely".[2] In Lent of 1671 he gave a course at Notre-Dame and Mme de Sévigné went regularly to hear either him or Mascaron the Oratorian. On Good Friday she heard Mascaron:

> J'ai entendu la passion de Mascaron, qui en vérité a été très belle et très touchante. J'avois grande envie de me jetter dans le Bourdaloue, mais l'impossibilité m'en ôte le goût: les laquais y étoient dès mercredi, et la presse étoit à mourir.

One could not have a stronger testimony to Bourdaloue's popularity with the world of fashion—not only from the fact of people sending their servants two days beforehand to secure places, but also from the familiar expression "dans le Bourdaloue".[3] Mme de Sévigné

---

[1] Racine was his pupil and in his testament expressed a wish that he should be buried at the foot of his grave at Port-Royal.
[2] 3 December 1670.   [3] 27 March (Good Friday) 1671.

uses it again on Christmas Day in the same year (1671), when he was preaching at Saint-Jean-en-Grève:

Je m'en vais en Bourdaloue; on dit que l'autre jours il fit trois points de la retraite de Tréville; il n'y manquoit que le nom, mais il n'en étoit pas besoin: avec tout cela on dit qu'il passe toutes les merveilles passées, et que personne n'a prêché jusqu'ici.

In spite of this remark and of the support given to it by Sainte-Beuve in his *causerie* on Bourdaloue,[1] I am disposed to agree with Feugère that it is not in accord with what we know of the great preacher that in the "portraits", as they were called, which he used in his sermons as illustrations of general truths, he should have portrayed living individuals.[2] But there is an almost certain portrait of Tréville, under the name of Arsène, in La Bruyère's *Caractères*,[3] and there is an admirable sketch of him by Saint-Simon.[4] His retreat from the world was caused by the sudden death of Mme Henriette, but he returned to it from time to time. His learning, his *esprit*, and his piety made him the centre of an admiring circle, but others resented the air of superiority which he invariably displayed.

Bourdaloue preached before the Court again in Lent of 1672, and in one sermon the Maréchal de Gramont was so moved that he suddenly said in a loud voice "Mordieu! il a raison". Madame, the second wife of the Duke of Orleans, burst out laughing and there

---

[1] *Causeries du Lundi*, IX, 283 f.
[2] A. Feugère, *Bourdaloue*, 5th ed. 1889, p. 366.
[3] *Ouvrages de l'esprit*.
[4] *Mémoires*, ed. Chéruel and Regnies, 100 f. See also Sainte-Beuve, *loc. cit.* pp. 281–290.

was a general commotion.[1] A year and eight months later Bourdaloue had to break to the Maréchal, who was a dear friend, the news of the death of his eldest son, the Comte de Guiche. The interview, of which the Duc de Bourbon, who was in part an eye-witness, gave an account at Mme de La Fayette's, is touchingly related by Mme de Sévigné.[2]

Two months later she makes a special reference to Bourdaloue's sermon for the Purification, with which he began, as was customary, his Lent course before the Court for 1674: "Il étoit d'une force à faire trembler les courtisans."[3] Her next reference to him is after a sermon which he preached in Lent 1680, again before the Court:[3]

Nous entendîmes, après-dîné, le sermon du Bourdaloue, qui frappe toujours comme un sourd, disant des vérités à bride abattue, parlant à tort et à travers contre l'adultère; sauve qui peut, il va toujours son chemin.[4]

In Lent 1683 he gave a course in her own parish, and she is as enthusiastic as ever.[5] Finally, in a letter to M. de Moulceau at Montpellier, where Bourdaloue had been sent on a special mission to convert the Huguenots of this headquarters of Protestantism in the south of France, she speaks of him both as a man and a preacher in most appreciative and expressive terms:

C'est par ces sortes d'endroits tout pleins de zèle et d'éloquence qu'il enleve et qu'il transporte; il m'a

[1] 13 April 1672. [2] 8 December 1673.
[3] 5 February 1674. [4] 29 March 1680.
[5] 5 March 1683 (to M. and Mme de Guitaut); also 9 and 20 April of the same year.

souvent ôté la respiration par l'extrême attention avec laquelle on est pendu à la force et à la justesse de ses discours, et je ne respirois que quand il lui plaisoit de les finir, pour recommencer un autre de la même beauté. Enfin je suis assurée que...vous êtes aussi charmé de l'esprit, de la bonté, de l'agrément, et de la facilité du P. Bourdaloue dans la vie civile et commune, que charmé et enchanté de ses sermons.[1]

In Lent of 1689 she heard a great many sermons for, as she explains, when the "great Pan" was not preaching, other preachers were listened to. She mentions especially Père Soanen,[2] an Oratorian, afterwards Bishop of Senez, whom Fénelon couples with Bourdaloue as the best model for a beginner, and Père Anselme, against whom she had at first been prejudiced, but whom she now regarded as an excellent preacher, inferior to none.[3] He had had a high reputation ever since he had preached before the King in 1683. Mme de Sévigné mentions the marvellous success of the Jesuit, Père Gaillard, at Saint-Germain l'Auxerrois, but she does not say that she had heard him herself. It was he, it will be remembered, who, when he was preaching at Fontainebleau, made way for the King to announce the capture of Philippsburg, and then continued his sermon with great effect.[4] It was he who, urged by Père La Chaise, undertook the delicate task of delivering the funeral oration for the Archbishop of Paris, Harlay de Champvallon, whose unedifying life had been ended by sudden death: "La célèbre jésuite prit son parti", says Saint-Simon, "il loua tout ce qui

[1] 3 April 1686. [2] 28 March 1689.
[3] 8 April 1689. [4] See above, p. 22.

méritoit de l'être, puis tourna court sur la morale. Il fit un chef-d'œuvre d'éloquence et de piété."[1]

On the difficult questions of Grace and Predestination Mme de Sévigné agreed rather with St Augustine and Calvin than with the Jesuits. Thus in a letter to her daughter of 21 June 1680, written after reading St Augustine's treatise on *La prédestination des Saints*, she says:

Je n'ai rien à vous répondre sur ce que dit Saint Augustin, sinon que je l'écoute et je l'entends, quand il me dit et me répète cinq cents fois, dans un même livre, que tout dépend donc, comme dit l'Apôtre, "non de celui qui veut, ni de celui qui court; mais de Dieu qui fait miséricorde à qui il lui plaît; que ce n'est point en considération d'aucun mérite que Dieu donne sa grace aux hommes, mais selon son bon plaisir.

She gives as an instance Mme de La Sablière,[2] entirely cured, she says, of a malady (her passion for La Fare, who had deserted her for the combined attractions of the Champmeslé and *bassette*), which for some time was supposed to be incurable.

Elle est dévote et vraiment dévote; elle fait un bon usage de son libre arbitre; mais n'est-ce pas Dieu qui a tourné son cœur? n'est-ce pas Dieu qui l'a fait vouloir?...n'est-ce pas Dieu qui l'a fait marcher et qui la soutient?...Si c'est cela que vous appellez le libre arbitre, ah! je le veux bien.

---

[1] I, 278. And see a letter of Mme de Coulanges to Mme de Sévigné (16 September 1695).

[2] The protectress of La Fontaine. He wrote a graceful poem, *Discours à Mme de La Sablière*, and the fable of *Le Corbeau, la Gazelle, la Tortue et le Rat* (XII, xv) is preceded by a long dedication to her.

Then in a later letter she describes how Mme de La Sablière, when she found that La Fare had deserted her, retired quietly from the world to the Hospice des Incurables, where she nursed the sick, was visited by her friends, and was always good company.

Voilà la route que Dieu avoit marquée à cette jolie femme....Sa grace saura bien vous préparer les chemins, les tours, les détours, les bassettes, les laideurs, l'orgueil, les chagrins, les malheurs, les grandeurs; tout sert, tout est mis en œuvre par ce grand ouvrier, qui fait toujours infailliblement tout ce qu'il lui plait.[1]

Earlier in the same letter she sets out the doctrine of the "sovereign will of God", as she reads it in St Paul and St Augustine:

Ils ne marchandent point à dire que Dieu dispose de ses créatures comme le potier; il en choisit, il en rejette....Il leur fait donc justice, quand il les laisse à cause du péché originel qui est le fondement de tout, et il fait miséricorde au petit nombre de ceux qu'il sauve par son fils.[2]

There, she says, are her respectful thoughts; but they do not prevent her from hoping that she is one of the chosen number, "après tant de grâces qui sont des préjugés et des fondements de cette confiance".[2]

Evidently in her theory of grace she follows St Augustine in starting from an abstract idea of the divine power:

Dieu règle toutes choses comme il veut qu'elles soient, et que la place que vous tenez dans l'univers, telle qu'elle est, pouvoit point être dérangée.

[1] 14 July 1680.
[2] The letters from 15 June to 14 July 1680 are very important for the understanding of Mme de Sévigné's religious views.

Over the altar of the chapel at Les Rochers was inscribed in letters of gold *Soli Deo honor et gloria*, and on it was a picture of the Virgin and a crucifix. She wants nothing more:

Je crois tout simplement et en un mot que l'ordre est la volonté de Dieu: quand les choses vont comme elles doivent aller, c'est sa volonté:...quand ses ouvrages sont beaux et parfaits, et quand ils sont monstrueux et horribles, tout est dans cette volonté; l'un n'est donc pas moins que l'autre dans l'ordre de la providence.[1]

The expression of her complete trust in God constantly recurs, especially in her later letters:

Je laisse tout dans les mains de Dieu: je ne trouve de soutien et d'appui contre le triste avenir que je regarde que la volonté de Dieu et sa providence.[2]

This was written in 1689 when the affairs of the Grignan family were troubling her sorely.

At the beginning of the following year (1690) they were in a desperate state. "Mon Dieu, que votre état est violent," she writes on 22 January, "qu'il est pressant ! et que j'y entre tout entière avec une véritable douleur." Then she adds that she herself is sadly bothered by her petty creditors, and that she does not know whether she can satisfy them, for she is *suffoquée* by having to pay shortly 5000 *francs*. She had need of all her trust in God, in this "année des grandes infamies". In a letter written in the summer she expresses it in simple and beautiful words:

Ce que j'ai seulement c'est d'être persuadée qu'il n'y aurait que cette soumission qui pût donner la paix à

[1] VI.   [2] IX.

notre cœur, et que nous devons la souhaiter, comme la chose du monde la plus chrétienne, et la plus convenable à la créature, à l'égard de son créateur et du maître de toutes choses.[1]

A little later than this, but also from Les Rochers, she wrote with reference to the jubilee which the new Pope (Alexander VIII) had proclaimed, and which she had kept at Vitré:

Je me jette aux pieds de Jésus-Christ, et m'abandonne à lui et pour les coulpes et pour les peines, me trouvant très-digne de toutes les peines qu'il voudra me faire souffrir, trop heureuse mille fois s'il ne me rejette point du nombre de ses enfants.

It was this belief in God and Jesus Christ that gave her courage to face *assez solidement* the last act of life. It was part of her creed that the hour and manner of a man's death was, like his life, pre-determined by God. She says of Mme Du Plessis-Guénégaud that "her hour was marked from all eternity", and similarly of Turenne that the cannon which caused his death was "loaded from all eternity". This sounds like an unbending fatalism, but it was really the expression of her belief in God's Providence and in her submission to His will. A really Christian death moved her strongly. Two of her most beautiful letters are those in which she recounts the last illness of her uncle, M. de Saint-Aubin,[2] who died in a house adjoining the Carmelite convent in the Faubourg Saint-Jacques, the house in which that

[1] Dated July, without mention of the year, but it evidently belongs to 1690. She kept the jubilee from June 24 to 26 (ed. Momerqué, IX, 556).

[2] 17 and 19 November 1688.

illustrious penitent, Mme de Longueville, lodged when
she was in Paris, and in which she died.

She had not always looked on death with such firm
composure. In one of the best-known passages of her
letters, in answer to a question from her daughter
whether she was still greatly in love with life, she
replies that though she finds in it cruel sorrows, death
is even less to her liking. Then there follows an eloquent
passage, in which she wonders what sort of death
awaits her, how she will appear before God, and whether
she is worthy of paradise, or hell: "Je m'abîme dans
ces pensées, et je trouve la mort si terrible, que je hais
plus la vie, parce qu'elle n'y mène que par les épines
qui s'y rencontrent."[1] It was these feelings that
prompted her to inscribe on her sun-dial the words,
Ultimam time.

Mme de Sévigné's determination to stay through the
winter at Les Rochers caused much disquiet to her
friends in Paris. Early in October Mme de La Fayette,
Mme de Lavardin, and Mme de Chaulnes, all wrote to
her that she must not spend the winter in Brittany
on any account. Mme de Chaulnes's letter was "a
volume; there was no end to it". Mme de La Fayette's
(6 October), which is perhaps the best known of the
comparatively few letters of hers that have come down
to us, is a striking example of her downrightness and
habit of coming to the point, and an equally striking
testimony to her deep affection for her friend:

Il est question, ma belle, qu'il ne faut point que vous
passiez l'hiver en Bretagne, à quelque prix que ce soit.

[1] 16 March 1672.

Vous êtes vieille, ces Rochers sont pleins de bois; les catarrhes et les fluxions vous accableront. Vous vous ennuierez, votre esprit deviendra triste et baissera.

Then she goes on to say that when she comes to Paris she is to stay with Mme de Chaulnes and have use of her carriage and horses. As for her debts, she will find at Paris a thousand crowns, which will be lent her without interest and which she can repay gradually, as she pleases.

Point de raisonnement là-dessus, point de paroles, ni de lettres perdues. Il faut venir; tout ce que vous m'écrivez, je ne le lirai seulement pas; en un mot, ma belle, il faut ou venir ou renoncer à mon amitié, à celle de Mme de Chaulnes et à celle de Mme de Lavardin.

Mme de Sévigné truly says that the letter is in the tone of *un arrêt du Conseil d'en haut* (the unofficial name for the *Conseil d'État*), but she adds that it is "d'une vivacité et d'une amitié qui m'a fait plaisir". But she did not give way. We have not her answer, but we know the tenor of it from her letter to Mme de Grignan. Adopting a tone of *badinage* she said that she would be only moderately bored at Les Rochers in the company of her son and his wife and her books, and that she would come to Paris in the summer and live in her own house, and without being in debt for a thousand crowns to a generous friend—it was Mme de Chaulnes —"dont la belle âme et le beau procède me presseront plus que tous les sergents du monde". Finally, she gave her word that she would not fall ill, or grow old or *radoter*, and that Mme de La Fayette, in spite of her threats, would always love her. Grateful though she was to her friends' affection and thoughtfulness, the proposal was in fact highly repugnant to her: "La belle proposition de n'être plus chez moi, d'être dépendante, de n'avoir point d'équipage, et de devoir mille écus."[1]

She sent Mme de La Fayette's letter on to Mme de Grignan, who was struck by the words "Vous êtes vieille". Mme de Sévigné says in reply to her that she herself was surprised by them because she did not feel any loss of power to suggest old age. Then follow some apposite reflections on the approach of old age, of that time when you must either make an effort to fight against growing infirmities or else die, "which is repugnant to nature": "Mais un retour à la volonté de Dieu, et à cette loi universelle qui nous est imposée, remet la raison à sa place, et fait prendre patience."[2]

In spite of her intention to return to Paris in the summer, she remained at Les Rochers till 3 October 1690 and from there went to Grignan, arriving on 21 October after a journey of 450 miles. She travelled by litter, which she found "very gay", as far as Lyons. Unfortunately we have for the year 1690 comparatively few of her letters. In the edition of the *Grands Écrivains de la France* the last dated letter to Mme de Grignan is of 27 August, and it is incomplete.[3] Happily the Dijon MS. discovered in 1872 contained six entirely new letters to her daughter for the year 1690 and ten

---

[1] 12 October 1689. She refers to it again in the new fragment of a letter of 27 August 1690 printed by Capmas, II, 461–463.

[2] 30 November 1689.

[3] For the complete letter see *Lettres inédites*, II, 453 ff.

others that were only known in part.[1] One of the earliest (19 April) is particularly interesting.[2] It shews that Mme de Sévigné's brilliance and vivacity as a letter-writer have in no way diminished. There is no sign of *radotage*. It also bears witness to the intelligence and courage which she brought to bear on the management of her estate.

She remained at Grignan till the end of 1691 when she brought her daughter with her to Paris. She returned to Grignan in the middle of May 1694, her daughter having preceded her by six weeks. The last of her letters that we have, written to the faithful Coulanges, is dated 29 March 1696. It was occasioned by the death at the age of twenty-seven of the Marquis de Blanchefort, the second son of Mme de Créquy, widow of that very able and distinguished general, the Maréchal de Créquy, and grandson of Mme Du Plessis-Bellière, and it contains the following beautiful expression of sympathy:

Cet aimable garçon disparoît en un moment, comme une fleur que le vent emporte....Où peut-on trouver des paroles pour dire ce que l'on pense de la douleur de ces deux mères, et pour leur faire entendre ce que nous pensons ici?

Early in the year (10 January) she wrote as follows to the Président de Moulceau:

Pour moi, je ne suis plus bonne à rien; j'ai fait mon rôle, et par mon goût je ne souhaiterais jamais une si longue vie; il est rare que la fin et la lie n'en soit humiliante; mais nous sommes heureux que ce soit la

---

[1] Capmas, II, 337–485.   [2] *Ib.* pp. 349 ff.

volonté de Dieu qui la règle, comme toutes les choses de ce monde: tout est mieux entre ses mains qu'entre les nôtres.

When she wrote this letter, her beloved daughter was, and had been for some months, seriously, though not dangerously, ill. Hence the note of sadness. But it reads like a premonition. She died, after an illness of eleven days, on 17 April 1696, two and a half months after her seventieth birthday. "Elle a envisagé dès les premiers jours de sa maladie, la mort," writes the Comte de Grignan to the Président de Moulceau, "avec une fermeté et une soumission étonnantes."

IV

MME DE SÉVIGNÉ & HER BOOKS

As we have seen, Mme de Sévigné spent part of her day at Les Rochers in solitude and meditation. But she was seldom absolutely idle. In summer between five o'clock and supper she walked in her alleys and meditated on God and His Providence, but she took a book with her, and in autumn, after she had come in from her walk, her son read aloud, while she worked at her tapestry. When her friends told her that she would be bored to death if she stayed at Les Rochers through the winter, she replied that she had not only her son and her daughter-in-law but her books for companions. She not only read widely, but she read intelligently. When it was history she lived in imagination in the past, when it was theology or a work of devotion she pondered carefully over the arguments and took to heart the practical advice. She had an unusually good verbal memory, and the frequency with which she introduces quotations from her favourite authors, especially from Corneille, Pascal, Molière, and La Fontaine, is remarkable. The books that she read, and particularly the masterpieces of the day, were in fact so thoroughly assimilated in her mind that references or allusions to them sprang spontaneously to her pen. I cannot think of any other famous letter-writer who can be compared to her in this respect. In Gray, for instance, who was one of the most widely read men of his time, you will not find more than half-a-dozen quotations in a hundred letters. Mme Du Deffand, Mme de Sévigné's eighteenth-century successor—*longo intervallo*—was also a wide reader, and, though she says she had a bad memory, she whiled away weary hours of sleeplessness by repeating to herself long passages of *Esther*, *Athalie*—for her the one perfect work—and Voltaire. But though she often discusses literature both with Voltaire and with Horace Walpole, her literary quotations and references are even rarer than Gray's. Of course in Lamb's letters there are many more references to literary works than in Mme de Sévigné's, for he was steeped in literature himself, and he had as correspondents Coleridge, Wordsworth, Southey, and Hazlitt, not to speak of lesser lights like Crabbe Robinson, Bernard Barton, B. W. Proctor, Serjeant Talfourd, and H. F. Cary, the translator of Dante. But his references to literature are chiefly by way of appreciation or criticism and he hardly ever quotes passages in illustration of passing events in the spontaneous way of Mme de Sévigné's.

"Montaigne is an old friend", writes Mme de Sévigné from Livry in 1679 when she finds that she has unawares brought a copy with her. "Ah, l'aimable homme ! qu'il est de bonne compagnie", and she adds that she cannot read without tears in her eyes how Blaise de Montluc (the celebrated memoir-writer and soldier of the sixteenth century), having lost a promising son, regretted that he had never opened himself out to him but had left him ignorant of the tenderness that he felt for him. The story occurs in the essay dedicated to

Mme d'Estissac and entitled *De l'affection des pères aux enfants* (II, viii) and the fact that Mme de Sévigné substitutes *De l'amour des pères envers leurs enfants* shews that she is speaking from memory and not with the book before her. Her final remark is: "Mon Dieu que ce livre est plein de mon sens." Three years earlier she had written:

Montaigne est raccomodé avec moi sur beaucoup de chapitres: j'en trouve d'admirables et d'inimitables, et d'autres puériles extravagans; je ne m'en dédis point.

Two essays which must have given her great pleasure are *Des livres* (II, x) and *De trois commerces* (III, iii). She would have agreed more or less with the essayist when he says:

Je ne cherche aux livres qu'à m'y donner du plaisir par un honneste amusement; ou, si j'estudie, je ne cherche que la science qui traite de la connoisance de moy mesmes, et qui m'instruise à bien mourir et à bien vivre.

Like Montaigne, Mme de Sévigné loved history and for much the same reason, that it adds to our knowledge of mankind. Without going so far as to prefer, as he does, in the Essay *De trois commerces*, the society of books to that of men and women, she would have warmly endorsed his love of them and could have said with him, "Je ne voyage sans livres." Like him, though she delighted in company and conversation, she sometimes felt the need of solitude; but would she have gone so far as to say that "she found it more supportable to be always alone than to be never able to be alone"? Her love of Montaigne is particularly

interesting because from 1669, when two editions of
his Essays were published, his popularity and influence
in France had greatly declined. In a sermon preached
before the Court on All Saints' Day of that very year
Bossuet eloquently attacked his *Apologie de Raimond
Sebond*, and in 1674, only five years before Mme de
Sévigné's letter from Livry, Malebranche in his *Recherche
de la Vérité* criticised Montaigne's whole book most
harshly and unjustly. But earlier in the century he was
widely read and had great influence, especially in the
salon of Mme de Sablé before she became an ardent
disciple of Port-Royal—that is to say from about 1650
to 1660. It was probably in this salon, or at any rate
through common friends, that Pascal came under Montaigne's spell. Among its frequenters was La Rochefoucauld, who had grown up in a society deeply
affected by free-thought, and who was therefore already
an admirer of Montaigne. And Mme de La Fayette
once expressed a wish that she had him for a neighbour. It is not therefore surprising that Mme de
Sévigné should have shared the admiration of her two
intimate friends.

As a woman, she would have found a great deal to
her distaste in Rabelais, but on one occasion at Les
Rochers Charles read aloud some chapters of *Gargantua*
and *Pantagruel*, which made her "die of laughter". She
cites him twice, and follows up one of her quotations
with "Je tiens ceci d'un bon auteur", and she says
that the motto of Les Rochers was "Fay ce que
voudras". The only other sixteenth-century writers
that she seems to have read were translators—Herberay

des Essarts, the translator of *Amadis de Gaule*, and Amyot, the translator of Plutarch, but she does not mention them by name. Writing to Bussy on 20 July 1679 she says that her letter resembles the chapters of *Amadis*. Then she quotes the heading of one and adds:

Je suis tellement libertine, quand j'écris, que le premier tour que je prends règne tout au long de la lettre. Il seroit à souhaiter que ma pauvre plume galopant comme elle fait, galopât au moins sur le bon pied.

The reason for this comparison with *Amadis* is that she had said in her letter that the Bishop of Autun would tell Bussy *how* so and so had done this and *how* this had happened and *how*, etc., which is the way in which nearly all the chapters of *Amadis* are headed. Des Essarts has many of Mme de Sévigné's merits—variety, power both of description and narrative, choice of the most expressive word, and generally the art of carrying his readers along with him. His style "gallops" like Mme de Sévigné's, and like hers it "gallops smoothly". To the end of her life Mme de Sévigné retained her interest in *Amadis* and there are no less than six references in her letters to the *gloire de Niquée*. To Amyot's *Plutarch* I shall refer later.

Ronsard had fallen out of favour before she was born, but Marot still had readers, notably La Fontaine. In 1676 her friend Benserade turned Ovid's *Metamorphoses* into *rondeaux* after the pattern of Marot's, and Mme de Sévigné refers to his work. It is a pity that he did not persuade her to read his model, for she would almost certainly have appreciated him. The lyric poetry of her own century does not seem to have had much attraction for her. Ménage gave her a copy of Malherbe's poems, but she only quotes from him once. Her one quotation from Saint-Amant has been already mentioned. There is nothing from Théophile and only two lines—from *Les Bergeries*—from Racan. With Mme Deshoulières, nearly twelve years her junior, she had a personal acquaintance, and at the end of 1688 she sends her daughter some lines of hers with the remark that she would find them *bien faits*. The verses of Voiture, Sarasin, and Benserade, all frequenters of the Hôtel de Rambouillet, were familiar to her, but she probably would have said of all three what she said of Benserade: "Ses vers sont mêlés: avec un crible il en demeureroit peu." She quotes (three times) the last line—*J'en connois de plus misérables*—of his famous sonnet on Job, which with Voiture's rival sonnet to Uranie, in the year 1650, divided French society into Jobelins and Uranistes, and she quotes two lines from a poem by Voiture. Of the latter's letters she speaks with respect and admiration, and she reproaches her daughter for comparing her own letters with them.[1] As for Segrais, Voiture's rival as a wit and a poet, she had a copy of his works (1656 or 1658) and was reading them at Les Rochers in 1680.

With *L'Astrée*, Honoré d'Urfé's famous romance, which had so marked an influence on the Hôtel de Rambouillet, and of which the fourth and last authentic part appeared in 1627, the year after Mme de Sévigné's birth, she was evidently well acquainted. We find in

[1] Letter of 15 February 1690.

8-2

her letters references to the shepherds and shepherdesses of the river Lignon and to the Druid Adamas. Though she read the romances of D'Urfé's successors, the only one that really appealed to her was La Calprenède's *Cléopâtre*, which appeared from 1648 to 1660. "I dare not tell you", she writes to her daughter from Les Rochers in July 1671, "that I have returned to *Cléopâtre*" and she adds:

Par le bonheur que j'ai de n'avoir point de mémoire, cette lecture me divertit encore: cela est épouvantable: mais vous savez que je ne m'accomode guère bien de toutes les pruderies qui ne me sont pas naturelles; et comme celle de ne plus aimer ces livres-là ne m'est encore entièrement arrivée, je me laisse divertir sous le prétexte de mon fils qui m'a mise en train.

She loves, she says, to read about "les grands coups d'épée de l'invincible Artaban", and when Charles has left her she sets to work to finish it by herself: "Cela est d'une folie dont je vous demande le secret." It is true that she finds La Calprenède's style detestable, but "the beauty of the sentiments, the violence of the passions, the grandeur of the events, and the miraculous success of their redoubtable swords, transport her like a girl". For Mlle de Scudéry's novels in which the analysis of sentiment largely took the place of the *grands coups d'épée* she evidently cared much less, but she had read *Le Grand Cyrus* (1649–1653) and *Clélie* (1654–1660), and an incident in the campaign of 1672 reminds her of Oronte, a character in *Le Grand Cyrus*.[1] When Mlle de Scudéry sent her the first volumes

[1] 3 July 1672.

of her *Conversations* in 1688, she told her daughter that they were sure to be good now that they were no longer drowned in her great romance.[1] In June 1688 she writes to thank Mlle de Scudéry for her *Nouvelles Conversations*,[2] which had just been published. In 1676 she was reading a recently published novel entitled *Histoire des Grands Vizirs* by Champol which "all the world has read". She admits that it is not at all well written, but she found it interesting and she is glad that her daughter has read it.[3]

We now come to the three great names of her youth, to Corneille, Descartes, and Pascal. She was nine when *Le Cid* was produced, ten when *Le Discours de la Méthode* was published, and twenty-eight when the first Provincial Letter appeared. Her attitude towards Descartes's philosophy is characteristic. She did not profess to understand it or to be interested in it. That she left to her daughter, of whose reputation as a Cartesian she was evidently very proud. She always speaks of him in her letters as *votre père*:

Que ne demeurez-vous dans les droites simplicités de votre père? Il me faudra toujours quelque petite histoire; car je suis grossière comme votre père: les choses abstraites vous sont naturelles; comme elles nous sont étrangères.

Mme de Sévigné was quite right. She loved the concrete and she loved "little stories" about human nature. Moreover, believing as she did in the continual working

[1] 25 September 1680 (VII, 274).
[2] The letter is only dated *Mardi*, but it is evidently of the date indicated (VIII, 271).
[3] See letters of 15 May, 4 June and 12 August 1676.

of a loving Providence, she would have heartily agreed with Pascal's

Je ne puis pardonner à Descartes: il aurait bien voulu, dans toute sa philosophie, pouvoir se passer de Dieu: mais il n'a pu s'empêcher de lui faire donner une chiquenaude, pour mettre le monde en mouvement: après cela il n'a plus que faire de Dieu.

A niece of Descartes lived at Rennes, and Mme de Sévigné became very friendly with her for she had this virtue, that though she had seen very little of Mme de Grignan, she greatly admired her. "J'aime passionnément Mlle de Descartes," writes the fond mother, "celle vous adore." She was a friend of Mlle de Scudéry, and a *précieuse*.

Mme de Sévigné's enthusiasm for the *Lettres Provinciales* is so well known that little need be said about it here. The first Letter appeared (January 1656) shortly before Renaud de Sévigné went to live at Port-Royal, the last in May 1657, and the collected Letters in the following year. Thus their publication coincided with Mme de Sévigné's introduction to the Arnauld family, but though her friendship with them may have strengthened her interest in the Letters, she admired them from the first on their own merits. Her first mention of them is in a letter to Ménage written in September 1656, after reading the eleventh Letter, which was published on 18 August of that year. She speaks of it as *fort belle*. In her later letters there are references to individual Letters, and once she adapts to her own case Pascal's immortal remark at the close of the sixteenth Letter that "he had made it longer than usual because he had not had the time to make it shorter". But all her life she was constantly returning to the "Little Letters", rejoicing in their wit and eloquence and in the originality and perfection of their style, and enjoying them all the more because they were directed against the Jesuits. In the winter of 1689 her son read them aloud to her: "Bon Dieu, quel charme! et comme mon fils les lit!" And then for the benefit of her daughter, who complained that they were always the same thing, she sings their praises in words too well known to quote, in which she extols the delicate raillery of the first ten Letters and the serious and forceful eloquence of the last eight.[1]

There are not many references to the *Pensées*, which were first published in 1670. In September 1679 she quotes Pascal as saying that "all evils come from not knowing how to keep to one's room", and in one of her last letters, written to Mme Guitaut on 29 October 1692, she quotes *Dieu sensible au cœur* from the famous maxim:

C'est le cœur qui sent Dieu, et non la raison. Voilà ce que c'est la foi, Dieu sensible au cœur, non à la raison.

This was Mme de Sévigné's own deeply seated belief. It was far from being what is called fideism; it was the stay and guiding principle of her life.

Her enthusiasm for Corneille is as well known as her enthusiasm for the "Little Letters". Judging from her references to his plays, *Le Cid* was nearest to her heart, but *Polyeucte*, though she refers to it less often,

[1] 21 December 1689.

was not far behind. From both of these she quotes frequently, and evidently from memory. To *Cinna* and *Horace* there are nearly as many references as to *Polyeucte*, but there are fewer quotations from them. *Pompée*, which marks a long descent from its predecessor *Polyeucte*, is quoted four times, the same line twice; of *Rodogune*, which Corneille regarded as his best work, only half a line; and *Nicomède*, that interesting experiment, one line twice. Of the later plays, those which Corneille wrote after his return to the stage, the only one from which she quotes, and that only a line, is *Sertorius*, one of the best. Of *Œdipe*, the play which marked his return, and which he wrote on the encouragement of Foucquet, not a word, though it had a brilliant success. But she took a great interest in the production of *Pulchérie*, in which the love of the aged Martian for the chaste and cold heroine was said to be a reminiscence of the author's adventure with Mlle du Parc. In January 1672 Corneille read the play at La Rochefoucauld's house before Cardinal de Retz and other friends and Mme de Sévigné reports that it reminded her of "his lost vein".

Its production, however, did not take place till the following November. It was preceded by that of Racine's *Bajazet* (5 January 1672), which Mme de Sévigné went to see soon afterwards. She greatly admired Mlle de Champmeslé's acting, "She surpasses Mlle Desœillets"—who had died just before the production of *Bérénice*—by "cent mille piques", and "as for me, who am thought to be a good actress, I am not fit to light the candles when she appears". As for the play itself she thought it good—

rather involved towards the end, but full of passion and of a passion less insane than that of *Bérénice*: "But the great plays of Corneille are as much superior to those of Racine as his are superior to those of all the others."[1] Two months later, when her daughter had read the play, and had apparently praised it, she warns her against putting Racine on a par with Corneille: "Racine will never improve on *Alexandre* and *Andromaque*: *Bajazet* is inferior....He writes plays for the Champmeslé and not for posterity." Her other criticisms are too well known to repeat—Bajazet's glacial character, the non-observance of Turkish customs, "cette grande tuerie", and the lack of those "tirades de Corneille qui font frissonner". The dear lady is certainly prejudiced. She is prejudiced by her loyalty to the old dramatist who had charmed and thrilled her and her contemporaries in their young days. For she prided herself on her loyalty to her old friends, and she was all the more moved to champion Corneille because she recognised that he had lost his vein and that during the last twelve years he had produced no remarkable work. On the other hand, ever since *Bérénice—Britannicus*, that fine play, was not well received—Racine had gone on from triumph to triumph and he was on the eve of being elected to the Académie Française. There was a growing animosity between the admirers of the rival dramatists, which led to deliberate attempts to ruin the first performance of *Iphigénie* and *Phèdre*, and which in the case of the latter play succeeded. Though Mme de Sévigné had no share in these discreditable cabals, they

[1] 15 January 1672.

helped, no doubt, to strengthen her attachment to Corneille and to make her unjust to Racine. To couple *Alexandre*, in which Corneille's influence blends with Quinault's, with *Andromaque*, which by substituting ordinary men and women for heroes and supermen gave an entirely new direction to French classical drama, shews a decided want of insight. But apart from this and apart from prejudice, it is doubtful whether Racine's tragedy would greatly have appealed to Mme de Sévigné. Neither the marvellous skill with which Racine develops the characters of Agrippine and Néron, nor the noble portrayal of the conflict between passions and duty in Titus, Bérénice, and Antiochus aroused her admiration. Her judgments, to use Montaigne's word, were *primesautier*. She had not the patience to allow Racine's psychological subtleties to penetrate her mind; she preferred the glamour of Corneille's heroes and heroines, the excitement of his plots, and the thrill of his tirades. Yet *Phèdre*, which she never mentions, has a plot of intense passion, and in one scene alone (IV, 6) there are three speeches, which as spoken by Mlle Champmeslé might have thrilled her as much as any of Corneille's.

Her enthusiasm for the elder Corneille did not prejudice her in favour of his younger brother, Thomas, for she speaks contemptuously of his highly successful tragedy, *Ariane* (1672) as "une comédie fade". On the other hand Desmarets de Saint-Sorlin's *Les Visionnaires* (1637) gave her great pleasure. She thought it a true picture—it is in reality more of a caricature than Molière's *Les Précieuses ridicules*—because they all have their visions in a more or less marked form.[1] But in the years 1674 to 1677 her chief theatrical interest was in the opera, which at this time was enjoying a high popularity in the hands of Lully and Quinault. She does not mention their first production, *Cadmus et Hermione* (1673) but she calls *Alceste* (1674) "un prodige de beauté"[2] and she describes *Atys* (1676) at some length, and with much admiration for the scenery, the dresses, and the music: "Cependant on aime encore mieux *Alceste*." The next, *Isis* (1677), furnished her with nicknames, as we have seen, for the King's mistress, Mme de Ludres, whom she calls sometimes Isis and sometimes Io. When *Proserpine* was produced in 1680, her interest seems to have cooled, for she did not go and see it. But she heard that it was "parfaitement beau" and many persons who had seen it thought of her and her daughter. But she had not told her daughter before, because if she were Ceres and her daughter Proserpine, M. de Grignan was Pluto and he might answer in the words of one of the choruses, "Une mère vaut-elle un époux".[3] Of the other operas she mentions *Amadis* (1684) twice, but she makes no reference to *Armide*, which is generally regarded as Quinault's masterpiece.

Mme de Sévigné's reminiscences of Molière are as numerous and as spontaneous as those of Corneille. She refers to his characters as if they were living people. At Orleans, when the axle of her carriage broke, there came to her assistance "the veritable portrait of M. de

[1] 4 August 1677.   [2] 8 January 1674.
[3] 9 February and 1 March 1680.

Sotenville". He brought up his wife, who was certainly of the family of La Prudoterie, "ou le ventre ennoblit", and Mme de Sévigné spent two hours in their company without being wearied by their conversation. She makes two other references to M. and Mme de Sotenville—that immortal couple. As one might expect she frequently refers to Molière's doctors, whether generally as "the doctor of the comedy" or to specific examples, such as those of *L'Amour médecin*. One of her favourite plays was *Le Médecin malgré lui*, in which that amusing rascal Sganarelle, in his capacity of a sham doctor, ridicules the medical routine and jargon of his day with infinite verve. Mme de Sévigné quotes or refers to the play even more often than she does to *Tartuffe*, which, however, was evidently her favourite. In both these preferences it is interesting to note that she agrees with the popular verdict, for in the number of performances at the Comédie Française between 1680 and 1906 *Tartuffe* heads the list with 2111, *Le Médecin malgré lui* comes second with 1625, and *L'Avare* third with 1549. With Mme de Sévigné *L'École des Femmes* comes third with seven notices, *L'Avare* fourth with five, and then *Le Mariage forcé* and *L'Amour médecin* with four apiece. Others to which she refers or quotes from are *George Daudin*, in which M. and Mme Sotenville appear, *Le Malade imaginaire*, *L'École des Maris* and *Les Femmes savantes*. It must not be supposed of course that these references are more than a rough guide to her preferences. It must be in some measure a mere matter of chance which play comes into her head. Moreover, some of the plays, by reason of telling incident or witty sayings, lend themselves more naturally to quotation or come more pat to the memory than others. Among these would be *Tartuffe*, *L'Avare*, *L'École des Femmes* and I should have said *Le Bourgeois Gentilhomme*, which, however, is never mentioned by Mme de Sévigné. Another comedy, the absence of which surprises me, is *Les Précieuses ridicules*. She may not, like Mme de Rambouillet and her daughter, the first Mme de Grignan, have been among the *gens de toute qualité* who witnessed the first performance of that brilliantly successful comedy, but whether she saw it in its early days or read it first, when it was printed a year later, it must have moved her to inextinguishable laughter.

Two comedies which might have been mentioned in her letters, but are not, are *Amphitryon*, which, whenever Sosie appears, produces some of Molière's most highly comic scenes, and *Les Fourberies de Scapin*. *Don Juan* is only referred to once, and not by name, and *Le Misanthrope*, perhaps Molière's masterpiece, also only gets a bare mention. Is this last omission purely an accident, or does it, coupled with the fact that *Les Femmes savantes* is only referred to twice, indicate that Mme de Sévigné was not so sensitive to the high comedy of *Le Misanthrope* and *Les Femmes savantes* as to the broader effects of *Tartuffe* and *L'Avare*?

On 12 March 1671 Barbin, the well known Paris publisher, completed the printing of two new volumes by La Fontaine, entitled *Fables nouvelles et autres poésies* and *Contes et Nouvelles en vers, Troisième partie*, and on the following day Mme de Sévigné sent both volumes to her daughter. Six weeks later, writing from Livry, she says that at M. de La Rochefoucauld's—it was the day that they heard of Vatel's tragic end—they were entranced by the fables and had learnt by heart *Le Singe et le Chat* and then she quotes from it six lines quite correctly: "Cela est peint: et *la citrouille* et *le rossignol*, cela est digne du premier volume." *Le Gland et la Citrouille* (IX, 4), which is a defence of the ways of Providence, would have specially appealed to her. The volume contained eight new fables, which were afterwards distributed among Books VII to IX. None of them, except one, not even the well known *Le Singe et le Chat*, though they are all good, are among La Fontaine's greatest achievements. The exception is *Le Coche et la Mouche* with its wonderful picture of the coach and its six strong horses toiling up the hill on a bad road in full sun, and the passengers, women, old men, and a monk, walking after it. Of this fable Mme de Sévigné, who in a much later letter compares herself to the importunate fly, might well have said, "Cela est peint." A month later, writing from Malicorne on her way to Les Rochers, she makes a witty reference, with a quotation, to La Fontaine's fine fable, *L'Aigle et le Hibou* (v, xviii). Altogether she refers to about twenty fables. Two of her references are especially interesting, because they are to fables which were not published till several years later. Writing on 9 March 1672 the letter already referred to, in which she speaks of the reading of *Pulchérie* before the Cardinal de Retz, she refers to the fable of *Le Curé et le Mort* (VII, x) being founded on the death of M. de Bouffler's *Curé* under similar circumstances a fortnight earlier. "La fable est jolie," she adds, "mais ce n'est rien au prix de celles qui suivront. Je ne sais ce que c'est que ce *pot au lait*." The fable in fact ends with the words "la fable du Pot au lait", and when La Fontaine's volume containing books VII to XI appeared in 1678 this famous fable preceded that of *Le Curé et le Mort*.

That La Fontaine should have sent Mme de Sévigné a copy of it in manuscript is not surprising, for he was on friendly terms not only with her, whom he must often have met in the days when he was in Foucquet's service, but also with La Rochefoucauld, for whom he wrote the fable of the First Book entitled *L'Homme et son Image*, and with Mme de La Fayette to whom he sent a small billiard-table with an epistle in verse. Mme de Sévigné also had an indirect share in the Fables, for the first of the Fourth Book, *Le Lion amoureux*, is addressed to her daughter:

> Sevigné, de qui les attraits
> Servent aux graces de modele,
> Et qui naquistes toute belle,
> A vostre indifference prés.

The next volume of Fables, containing Books VII to XI, did not appear till 1678. It opens with the great fable of *Les Animaux Malades de la Peste*. Of this Mme de Sévigné cites a line,

Ils ne mouroient pas tous, mais tous étoient frappés,

to describe the colds from which all Paris was suffering.

Her love of La Fontaine is not surprising; they were in many ways kindred spirits and had many qualities in common—love of nature, humour, descriptive power in a high degree, and, above all, an imagination which shewed itself not only in creation but also in expression. Like Molière and Bossuet they belonged rather to the age of Louis XIII than to that of Louis XIV, to an age when the language had not been brought under complete control, pruned, and polished by the Hôtel de Rambouillet and the Académie Francaise. They wrote, not according to strict rule, but at the spontaneous promptings of their own genius. They did not shrink from an unusual word: they would even "offend", if not "grammar", at any rate syntax.

With Boileau, as with La Fontaine, Mme de Sévigné was personally acquainted. In September 1680 she was reading his *Œuvres diverses* (1674), which included all his *Satires*, *Epistles* i–iv, the *Art Poétique*, and the first four books of *Le Lutrin*. She quotes in her letters from Satires i and ii, altering the quotations to suit her application of them, and from iv and ix (*le clinquant de Tasse*). She also makes two quotations from *Le Lutrin* and one allusion to it. Writing on 15 December 1673 she relates that at a dinner-party at Gourville's, the evening before, the *Art Poétique* was read, that is to say some months before it appeared in print. She adds that "it is a *chef-d'œuvre*". The rest of the *Epistles* (except xvi) and *Le Lutrin* were published in 1683, but she makes no reference to them. At a considerably later date (1690) she tells in an inimitable way the story of Despréaux—as he was always called by his contemporaries—and the Jesuit at a dinner with M. de Lamoignon, the distinguished Advocate-General, to whom Boileau's Sixth Epistle is addressed.[1] Bourdaloue

[1] See above, pp. 49–50.

and Corbinelli were also of the party. Mme de Sévigné's story is too well known for repetition, but the point of it is that in the course of a discussion on the relative merits of the ancients and the moderns—the first volume of Perrault's *Parallèle* had appeared—Boileau had maintained that there was one modern who, in his opinion, surpassed all the ancients and all the moderns, and that when the Jesuit asked him to name this marvellous author, he at first declined, but on being pressed, took hold of the Jesuit's arm and said, "Mon Père, vous le voulez; hé bien! morbleu, c'est Pascal." The Jesuit became very red: Boileau shouted like a madman; the Jesuit became furious; and Boileau, taking Corbinelli by the arm, fled to the other end of the room.[1]

When Bossuet was appointed tutor to the Dauphin, in 1670, he ceased preaching in Paris. That is to say, he no longer gave regular courses in Advent and Lent. But on 4 June 1675 he preached the sermon at the profession of Mme de La Vallière, and Mme de Sévigné, who did not hear it, reports that it was considered "not as divine as had been expected".[2] She did not hear either the last and greatest of his funeral orations, that on Condé, with its touching final words of farewell— "je réserve au troupeau que je dois nourrir de ma parole les restes d'une voix qui tombe et d'une ardeur qui s'éteint"—but she writes to Bussy on the same day (10 March 1687) that she had just seen a bishop who was present and that he said that M. de Meaux "had surpassed himself". The *Oraisons funèbres* were published as a whole in 1689 and Mme de Sévigné read

[1] Letter of 15 January 1690. [2] 5 June 1675.

them in the following January, together with separate orations by Mascaron, Fléchier, and Bourdaloue:

Nous repleurons M. de Turenne, Mme de Montausier, M. le Prince, feue Madame, la Reine d'Angleterre, nous admirons ce portrait de Cromwel; ce sont des chef-d'œuvres d'éloquence qui charment l'esprit: il ne faut point dire, oh! cela est vieux; non, cela n'est point vieux, cela est divin.[1]

Mascaron and Fléchier both established their reputations by funeral orations on Turenne. Mme de Sévigné did not hear Fléchier's, but when it was read to her by Mme de Lavardin she liked it better than Mascaron's.[2] Yet she had thought the latter admirable[3] when it was delivered in October 1675 at the great Paris convent of the Carmelites, where Turenne's heart was deposited. As General Weygand points out, the Duchesse de Longueville, for whom Turenne's heart had once beaten, must also have heard it. The oration on Mme de Montausier, the celebrated Julie d'Angennes, who died in November 1671, was also delivered by Fléchier, but Mme de Sévigné was absent from Paris at the time. His oration on Turenne may be "plus également belle partout" than Mascaron's, but it is pure declamation, whereas the third part of his rival's, which treats of Turenne's conversion, is really impressive. Mascaron preached his Lent course of 1671 at St Paul's, Mme de Sévigné's parish church, and paid her a visit. Consequently she thought it the duty of "une vraie petite

[1] 11 January 1690.
[2] 28 March 1676. His oration was delivered in January 1676 at St Eustache.
[3] 10 November 1675.

dévote" to ask him to dinner. As he was a native of Marseilles, they found an agreeable topic of conversation in Provence.[1] Of the two orations of Bossuet's that she mentions, besides the one on Condé (M. le Prince), that on Henriette d'Angleterre is a possible rival to the latter, while that on her mother, Henrietta Maria, contains the portrait of Cromwell—"homme... d'une profondeur d'esprit, hypocrite raffiné autant qu'habile politique"—which Mme de Sévigné as a Frenchwoman and a believer in divine right duly admired.

Bourdaloue, whose severe style of oratory was seldom warmed by emotion or imagination, was not at home in funeral panegyrics. But Mme de Sévigné, who heard him deliver his oration on Condé, would probably not have admitted it was inferior to Bossuet's. In a letter to Bussy[2] she uses the consecrated phrase, "he surpassed himself", and then proceeds to give a short *résumé*. She longs to see it printed, as that of M. de Meaux already is. The latter is "fort belle et de main de maître", but she thinks the famous parallel between Condé and Turenne "un peu violent". It required indeed much courage to compare a prince of the blood with an ordinary nobleman, whose family was not in high favour, and Mme de Sévigné and her friends evidently thought the comparison unbecoming. To the modern reader it seems magnificent. Bourdaloue is certainly not altogether at his ease in the first two parts

---

[1] I, 83 (11 March 1671).
[2] Letter dated 25 April 1687, but not sent till after the oration was delivered on 26 April.

of his oration, and in particular he does not deal with Condé's military career in the same masterly fashion as Bossuet. But when he comes in the third part to speak of his conversion from religious indifference to a convinced belief and an active religious life, his absolute sincerity arrests and keeps our attention. He is no longer the panegyrist of a great soldier, he is a Christian pastor rejoicing over a strayed sheep that has returned to the fold.

In the summer of 1689 Mme de Sévigné was reading Bossuet's *Histoire des Variations des Églises Protestantes*, published in the previous year—"ah, le beau livre à mon gré!"—and she was still reading it in the following November.[1]

Since she did not pretend to understand Descartes, she was not likely to be attracted by his disciple, Malebranche. She did not read *La Recherche de la Vérité* (1674-1675) itself—"Bon Dieu! je ne l'entendrais pas"—but she read a little book of conversations extracted from it, and in some letters of July and August 1680 she criticises some of the statements of "votre père Malebranche" in a gently mocking spirit.[2]

Mme de Sévigné's attitude towards the works of her friends La Rochefoucauld and Mme de La Fayette has a special interest. During the thirteen years which elapsed from the publication of the first authorised edition of the *Maximes* to the last edition published in the author's lifetime (1678), when the maxims mounted up from 314 to 514, she must have been present at

[1] 1 June 1689 and 23 November 1689.
[2] 2, 7 and 31 July, 4 August.

many discussions of them at the Hôtel de La Roche-foucauld or in the Rue de Vaugirard. But though she must have admired the perfection of their style and the knowledge of the world—of her own and La Roche-foucauld's world—that they display, she evidently did not take them to her heart or regard them with any particular enthusiasm. On 20 January 1672 she sends her daughter the latest edition—the third authorised edition, which was published in 1671 and which contained 341 maxims—and she adds: "Il y en a de divines, et à ma honte il y en a que je n'entends point; Dieu sait comme vous les entendrez." In other letters she occasionally questions the truth of some particular maxim, or suggests a variation in its wording. When we remember that Mme de La Fayette, who certainly took a less favourable view of human nature than her friend, was shocked at the general corruption that they revealed, it is not surprising that Mme de Sévigné should also have been repelled by the pessimism and cynicism that characterise many of them, and that even a further acquaintance did not altogether reconcile her to them. For she did not take as keen a psychological interest as her friend in the many problems and cross-currents that arose from loveless marriages in a society whose standard of conjugal fidelity was decidedly low. She had no *Princesse de Clèves* before her.

On 18 March 1678 she announces the arrival of this masterpiece to her cousin Bussy—"une des plus char-mantes choses que j'ai jamais lues"—and she asks him for his opinion of it. He took his time, and three months later she asks him again. His criticism, when it came, was that the first part was admirable, but that the second was not so good. Arguing from his own experience as a libertine, he thought it unnatural that Mme de Clèves should have told her husband that she loved M. de Nemours, still more unnatural that loving him she should have resisted him, and most unnatural of all that after her husband's death she should have refused to marry him. Thus he misses the whole beauty and originality of the story, which is that of the struggle between passion and virtue in a woman who is as true to herself as she is to her husband.

It is a surprise and a disappointment to find that Mme de Sévigné agrees with him. She must have known her cousin's character and history well enough to see that he was incapable of judging how a woman like the Princesse de Clèves would act under the circumstances. But, apart from Bussy's influence, I doubt whether she was of a nature to appreciate fully her friend's masterpiece. We have seen that neither Racine's subtle interpretation of character, nor his masterly portrayal of the inner conflict of souls, as revealed in *Britannicus*, *Bérénice*, and *Phèdre*, appealed to her, and Mme de La Fayette the novelist, though necessarily by different methods, worked to the same end as Racine the dramatist. Both alike were creative psychologists. Mme de Sévigné could admire their creative genius, but she did not take much interest in their psychology.

Far different was her attitude towards Nicole, whom she was also reading in the same summer of 1680, specially commending to her daughter his essay *De la soumission à la volonté de Dieu*. This was by no means her first introduction to the *Essais de Morale*, for there are many references to them in the letters written from Les Rochers in the autumn of 1671, the year in which they began to appear.

> Je poursuis cette *morale* de Nicole, que je trouve délicieuse; elle ne m'a encore donné une leçon contre la pluie, mais j'en attends; car j'y trouve tout.[1]

A week later she writes that she is particularly charmed with *Des moyens de conserver la paix avec les hommes*. This is the treatise to which Voltaire calls special attention in his notice of the author in *Les Écrivains du Siècle de Louis XIV* as "un chef-d'œuvre auquel on ne trouve rien d'égal en ce genre dans l'antiquité". She was reading him throughout the winter of 1676 and she is delighted to find that her daughter shares her admiration:

> Vous me ravissez d'aimer les *Essais de morale*; n'avois-je pas bien dit que c'étoit votre fait?...Quel langage! quelle force dans l'arrangement des mots! on croit n'avoir lu de françois qu'en ce livre.[2]

She never grew tired of Nicole, and during her long last sojourn at Les Rochers in 1689 and 1690 he was her constant companion. In October 1689 she writes to Mme de Grignan:

> A propos des livres, vous dîtes des merveilles des derniers de M. Nicole; j'en ai lu des endroits qui m'on paru très beaux; le style de l'auteur éclaire, comme vous dîtes, et nous fait rentrer dans nous-mêmes d'une manière qui découvre la beauté de son esprit et la bonté de son cœur.[3]

23 September 1671.   [2] 12 January 1676.   [3] 26 October 1689.

There was one member of the family, however, who did not share this enthusiasm. With his mother's letter of 12 January 1676 Charles encloses one of his own, in which he says:

Pour les *Essais de morale*, je vous demande très-humblement pardon si je vous dis que le *Traité de la connoissance de soi-même* me paroît distillé, sophistique galimatias en quelques endroits, et sur-tout ennuyeux presque d'un bout à l'autre.... Vous qui aimez tant les bons styles... pouvez-vous mettre en comparaison le style de Port-Royal avec celui de M. Pascal? C'est celui qui dégoûte de tous les autres: M. Nicole met une quantité de belles paroles dans le sien; cela fatigue et fait mal à la fin; c'est comme qui mangeroit trop de blanc-manger.

The epithets which Charles applies to Nicole's work are not perhaps well chosen, except that of *ennuyeux*, but his comparison of the style of Port-Royal with that of Pascal is very much to the point. Port-Royal had done good service to French prose, and in the direction of correctness and clarity had carried it to a point beyond the prose of Descartes. But, as Bossuet says, the style of the Port-Royalists in general lacks variety and charm. It is monotonous and what the French call *triste*. This is the fault alike of Arnauld and Nicole, their two greatest writers—for as regards style one does not think of Racine any more than Pascal as a Port-Royalist. "The phrase of Arnauld", says Brunetière, contrasting it with Pascal's, "was like that of Descartes, only clarified by a white and cold light, everywhere the same and uniformly diffused." This is equally true of Nicole. "His expression is clear, firm, and absolutely correct, but there is never any novelty in it." This is what Sainte-Beuve says, not, indeed, of Nicole, but of Bourda- loue—a Jesuit, but a Jesuit whose sermons have all the austerity of Jansenism—and he adds, "C'est un Nicole éloquent, a-t-on dit." As a fact, his remarks fit Nicole better than Bourdaloue, and in consequence no one reads him nowadays any more than they read Arnauld. But it must be remembered that right down to the middle of the eighteenth century he was greatly read and admired. Of the *Essais de Morale* alone exactly a hundred editions between their first publication and 1757 are recorded in the catalogue of the *Bibliothèque Nationale*. We have seen that Voltaire admired them, butr what seems more surprising is that Mme Du Deffa d, who was bored with nearly everybody and everything, writing to her friend Mme de Choiseul in 1765, says that for the last month she had read two chapters of Nicole every day: "Je le trouvais un bon raisonneur, il me faisait quelque bien."

It was for a somewhat similar reason that Mme de Sévigné was attracted to Nicole. In the letter quoted above she gives it in a single sentence: "Il nous fait rentrer dans nous-mêmes." A true child of her age, she was deeply interested in moral questions, especially from the point of view of her own conduct, and like her contemporaries she found what she wanted in Bourdaloue and Nicole. To us Nicole seems common- place and monotonous, whereas Bourdaloue holds our attention, not only by his oratorical feeling for move- ment, but also by his straightforward sincerity and the profound knowledge of human nature that he had gained from his long experience as a confessor. But his sermons were not printed in Mme de Sévigné's lifetime, whereas new volumes of Nicole were constantly appearing. She could meditate on them at her leisure as she walked in her beloved alleys.

Soon after arriving at Les Rochers in the early summer of 1680 she writes to her daughter that she has been arranging a quantity of books that she had brought with her.[1] One shelf is given up to books of devotion, another to history, a third to morals, and a fourth to poetry, tales, and memoirs. It will be noticed how greatly serious books preponderate and that history has a whole shelf. In this subject she read widely, ranging over many countries and many centuries. She read Tacitus, not in one of Perrot d'Ablancourt's *belles infidèles* but in the original, and she reminds her daughter how, when they read him together, she often interrupted the reading in order to point out to her the harmony of some special passage,[2] and a fortnight later she asks her if she can have the cruelty not to finish Tacitus: "Will you leave Germanicus in the middle of his conquests?" In the autumn of November 1675 she read Josephus's *History of the Jewish War* in her old friend Arnauld d'Andilly's agreeably written but not very faithful translation.[3] She is delighted to find that her daughter likes it and she encourages her to persevere till the siege of Jotopata, which Josephus, who commanded in person, relates with extraordinary minute-

[1] Letter of 5 June 1680.
[2] Letter from Les Rochers of 28 June 1671.
[3] 5 and 6 November 1675.

ness of detail, and that of Jerusalem, where the historian was also present though not in command.[1] And she adds, "Ah! que l'on pleure Aristobule et Marianne." Their deaths, both by order of Herod the Great, Marianne's husband, are related in *The Jewish Antiquities*, and Marianne is the subject of Hardy's unliterary but dramatic play of that name, which opens with the appearance of Aristobulus's ghost. Mme de Sévigné had now turned to French history in order to read about the crusades, but she does not find the account of them comparable to Josephus's narrative. At a rather later date[2] she again met with the first crusaders in an abridged translation of Anna Comnena's *Alexiad* (the biography of her father, the Emperor Alexius) by Louis Cousin, a President of the Cour des Monnaies.[3] The princess Anna, it will be remembered, plays an important part in Sir Walter Scott's *Count Robert of Paris* and the incident of the Frankish Count (Count Robert) seating himself in the Emperor's throne is taken from the *Alexiad*.

In her later years, that is to say in the winter of 1689, she speaks of having read the *Life of Saint Louis*. Is she referring to Joinville's *Mémoires*, the third edition of which, edited by Ducange, had appeared in 1668? If so one would have liked to know what she thought of this admirable work, in which the interest of its saintly hero's life is invested with an incomparable charm by the personality of his faithful companion-at-

---

[1] 5 and 6 November 1675.   [2] 18 August 1672.
[3] In *Histoire de Constantinople*, 8 vols. 1672, made up of extracts, translated from various Greek authors. Cousin was born in the same year as Mme de Sévigné.

arms. From the *Life of Saint-Louis* she was led to Mézeray in order to read about St Louis's successors, the last kings of the second race, and of Philip of Valois and his son John, the two feeble monarchs who began the new line.[1] Mézeray, whose work was published in 1643–1651, is not a trustworthy historian, but his literary conception of history would have appealed to Mme de Sévigné, as it did to her contemporaries. She doubtless knew her French history down to her own day, and she occasionally exchanges comments on historical events with Bussy. She expresses, for instance, her liking for the Gascon brigand-hero, La Hire, who as the knave of hearts retained his hold on popular affection for many years. In another letter to Bussy she refers to a quotation from Commines which he had sent her, but it is not clear that she herself possessed the *Mémoires*.

Of works by historians of her own day she mentions Vertot's successful *Histoire de la Conjuration de Portugal*, which she read in November 1689, five months after its publication, and found *fort belle*, and, in the same letter,[2] Maimbourg's *Histoire de l'Arianisme* (1672). She hates the author for his disagreeable style, but she reads some parts of his work with pleasure, as, for instance, his account of the Council of Nicæa. Of Bossuet's *Histoire des Variations* I have already spoken. Another solid work that engaged her attention was the *De la Vérité de la Religion chrétienne* by Jacques Abbadie, the well-known Protestant theologian, who accompanied Marshal Schomberg to England and later became

[1] 5 January 1689.   [2] 23 November 1689.

minister of the Huguenot church at the Savoy and Dean of Killaloe. On the other side of the great religious controversy she read *La Perpétuité de la Foi*, by "le grand" Arnauld. But she gave her greatest admiration and reverence to the man who was the fountain-head alike of Jansenism and Calvinism—St Augustine himself. On 21 October 1676 she says of his two treatises against the Pelagians, *De la prédestination des saints* and *Du don de persévérance*, French translations of which had been recently published, "C'est la plus belle et la plus hardie pièce qu'on puisse voir." A fortnight later she says, "Nous lisons toujours Saint-Augustin avec transport", and again in June 1680, "C'est un fort petit livre, il finit tout." Ten years later a friend sent her *De la véritable religion* and *Des mœurs de l'Eglise Catholique*, two of St Augustine's earliest treatises, which he wrote before he took priest's orders. Mme de Sévigné also read with great pleasure St Augustine's *Letters*,[1] which were translated into French in 1684 by Philippe Guibaud Du Bois. She read too the *Homilies* of St Chrysostom and found them divine.[2]

To return to purely historical works. She mentions a history of Brittany and an account of the discovery of America by Columbus. But she did not confine herself to French historians. She read Burnet's *History of the English Reformation* in a French translation which appeared in 1683–1685; Guicciardini's *Istoria d'Italia*; Davila's *History of the Civil Wars in France*, of which a fine edition was published at Paris in 1644; and

[1] 22 June 1690.   [2] 19 and 26 February 1690.

Herrera's *General History of the Indies*, which gave her extraordinary pleasure.

Enjoying as she did the biographical element in history she naturally delighted in biographies. She thought highly of Fléchier's *Life of Theodosius the Great*, she read a *Life of Becket*, and the *Life of Bertrand Du Guesclin*, by Paul Hay Du Chastelet, one of the first forty members of the Académie Française.

Of languages other than her own she read Italian with great ease, and Spanish with some difficulty. Latin she knew fairly well, but she was often glad to have a translation by her side. Her masters in these languages were Chapelain and Ménage, and from them she learnt Italian so thoroughly that she became in her turn a good teacher. Her pupil was the Abbé La Mousse, with whom she read Tasso at Les Rochers in the autumn of 1670–1671.[1] Tasso seems to have been her favourite Italian author, though Ariosto does not come far behind. She often refers to or quotes from both. She also read Petrarch and Guarini's *Il Pastor fido*, which was very popular in France at this time. Petrarch, Ariosto, Tasso, Guarini—these were the most read Italian writers in Mme de Sévigné's day, but Dante was practically ignored in France all through the seventeenth century. I have already mentioned the historians, Guicciardini and Davila. Spanish she evidently did not know so well. She read, as we have seen, Herrera, also Quevedo's *Visions*, of which there was a French translation, and, naturally, *Don Quixote*, but she says "that she was not so much in love with

[1] Letter of 21 November 1670.

the language as not to take pleasure in the translation".[1] The translation of the First Part appeared in 1614 and of the Second Part in 1618.

We have seen that she was sufficiently proficient in Latin to read Tacitus in the original, and to appreciate his language. She read the *Declamations* which passed under the name of Quintilian, but probably in a translation, either in that of Jean Nicole (1642) or in that of Bernard Du Theil (1659). She says that they amused her: "Il y en a de belles et d'autres qui m'ont ennuyée."[2] She also delighted in the great Latin poets. She quotes fairly often from Horace's *Odes* and *Satires*, but only once from the *Epistles*, and once from the *Ars Poetica*. She was familiar with the *Æneid*, from which she often quotes, but the *Georgics* only appear once in her letters, and the *Eclogues* not at all. In July 1672 she beguiled the tedium of the journey to Provence by reading Virgil with La Mousse, "non pas *travesti*, mais dans toute la majesté du latin et de l'italien".[3] She is referring to Annibale Caro's translation of the *Æneid* into blank verse (*versi sciolti*), which was published at Venice in 1581 and had a great success.

She did not know Greek, but she read Plutarch's moral treatises and was especially attracted by one entitled "Comment on peut discerner l'ami d'avec le flatteur", which is the title given to it in Amyot's translation. She read it for the second time in the winter of 1676 and was "more touched by it than when she read it first".[4] One would like to know what

[1] 26 August 1677.   [2] 13 October 1673.
[3] 16 July 1672.   [4] 12 January 1676.

she thought of Amyot's picturesque and redundant, but truly expressive, style. There is no mention of Plutarch's *Lives*, but one may feel sure that with her love of biography, she had read them. She certainly read Lucian, whose wit and satire she doubtless greatly appreciated. She only mentions Homer twice, once in an undated letter to Mme de Guitaut in which she says, "L'Odyssée m'est fort nécessaire."[1] Homer fared very badly in the French translations of the seventeenth century. The *Iliad* was translated by Souhait in 1614 (reprinted in 1617 and 1620), and the *Odyssey* in verse by Salomon Certon in 1604, and by Boitel in 1617. But after this Homer was neglected till Mme Dacier published her prose translation of the *Iliad* in 1711.

Mme de Sévigné judged books by the light of common sense and her personal impressions. But in accordance with the spirit of the age she liked to read works which bore on literary criticism, especially when they were well accredited not only by men of letters but by the reading public. Three writers of such works, all of about her own age, figure in her letters, and with all of them she was personally acquainted. I refer to the two Jesuit fathers, René Rapin and Dominique Bouhours, and to Le Bossu, a Canon regular of Sainte-Geneviève. She met Le Bossu at Livry in September 1676, and she reports to her daughter that he was "le plus savant homme qu'il est possible, et *Janseniste*".[2] In two letters of the following month she speaks of his *Art Poétique* as "fort admirée". She really means his

[1] xi, lxxiv.
[2] 16 September.

Traité du poème épique, which was published in 1675 and went through several editions. It was not till nearly four years later (May 1679) that she recounts a meeting with the two Jesuit fathers, Rapin and Bouhours. Of Rapin she says, "il me paraît un bon homme et un bon Religieux", and of Bouhours, "l'esprit lui sort de tous côtés".[1] Bouhours was red-faced and Rapin "paler than death", and when she got to know them better she accused Bouhours of having drunk his friend's blood. Rapin had a great reputation as a writer of Latin verse and his long poem on *Gardens* (1665–1666) was translated into English verse by John Evelyn. His French writings, which were very numerous, were mostly concerned with literary criticism. Mme de Sévigné mentions his *Instruction pour l'Histoire* (1677), which "seemed to her admirable", but the work by which he is best known, is *Réflexions sur la Poétique d'Aristote* (1675–1676). He died towards the end of October 1687, and in the following December Mme de Sévigné, writing to his friend Bussy, expresses her regret, and speaks of his goodness, his gentleness, and his great capacity.[2] Both he and Le Bossu had a great reputation in this country. Dryden praises them highly, and Congreve in his *Double Dealer* makes Brisk say to Lady Froth, "I presume your Ladyship has read Bossu", and her ladyship replies, "O yes, and Rapin and Dacier upon Aristotle and Horace."

Père Bouhours first came into prominent notice with his *Entretiens d'Ariste et d'Eugène* (1671), which

---

[1] 29 May 1679.
[2] 2 December 1687.

had a tremendous success.[1] The book provoked among other attacks one from Ménage, who spoke of him contemptuously as "un petit régent de troisième". The war between these guardians of the French language went on for some years and afforded much amusement to Mme de Sévigné. On 16 September 1676 she writes:

> Je lis...des livres de furie du Père Bouhours et de Ménage, qui s'arrachent des yeux, et qui nous divertissent. Ils se disent leurs vérités, et souvent ce sont des injures: il y a aussi des remarques sur la langue Française, qui sont fort bonnes; vous ne sauriez croire comme cette guerre est plaisante.

This was before she became acquainted with Bouhours. After they had become friends, he gave her a copy of his *Manière de bien penser sur les Ouvrages d'Esprit* (1687), a work which brought him even greater praise than the *Entretiens*. In the fifth edition of *Les Caractères*, published in 1690, La Bruyère put his name by the side of Bussy's as a writer of good French; Mme de Sévigné thought that Bouhours would have cited Bussy, but she can only find one place in which he gives his friend as an example. She says that she almost always agrees with his remarks and observations, whether of praise or blame, but that sometimes she "criticises his criticism".

The mention of La Bruyère reminds one that his name never occurs in Mme de Sévigné's letters. Yet his book, published at the beginning of 1688, had an

[1] Edited by M. René Radouant in the *Collection des Chefs-d'œuvre méconnus*, 1920.

immediate success, and by 1690 had reached a fifth edition. A book which proclaimed on its title-page that its subject was *Les Caractères et les Mœurs de ce Siècle* would, one would have thought, have proved peculiarly attractive to her, especially as the psychological analysis is not so subtle or profound as that of Racine or Mme de La Fayette. Moreover, she would have enjoyed the portraits and been diverted by the tone of satire or ridicule in many of the remarks. But it is noticeable that not only La Bruyère, but his contemporaries Bayle, Fénelon, Fontenelle, all of whom made their first appearance in literature after 1680, were equally unread, so far as one can judge from her letters, by Mme de Sévigné. It was hardly to be expected that she should know anything of Bayle, who had been living out of France since 1681, but she would have been interested in his *Pensées sur la Comète*—the great comet of 1680[1]—and disliking, as she did, the ex-Jesuit Maimbourg, she would have relished the lively controversy which Bayle carried on with him from 1682 to 1684. The articles in his *Nouvelles de la République des Lettres* (1684–1687) might not have appealed to her, though controversial theology, with which the majority of the book-reviews are concerned, always interested her. She only mentions Fontenelle once and merely as the author of an opera—*Bellérophon* (1679). Yet as early as 1683 he began to make his mark as a writer of prose literature with his *Dialogues des Morts*, and in 1686 he published two works which became very popular, *Entretiens sur la Pluralité des Mondes* and

[1] See her letters of 2 and 8 January 1680.

Histoire des Oracles. Neither of these was much in Mme de Sévigné's line, but she might have been tempted to look into them by the fact that the author was Corneille's nephew and strong partisan. The only work of Fénelon's that appeared in her lifetime was *Éducation des Filles* (1687). She does not refer to it, but she speaks of his appointment first as tutor to the Duc de Bourgogne and then as Archbishop of Cambrai. Of the former appointment she says that it is "divine".

The information that we get from Mme de Sévigné's letter about her literary tastes is of two kinds. First, we get references to the works that she had read in days before her correspondence with her daughter begins, that is largely to books which had become part and parcel of her mental outlook and which she knew so well that quotations from them come spontaneously to her pen. Secondly, there is the mention of books that she had recently read or was actually reading. Now it is obvious that the information under this second head is very incomplete. We know from her letters that when she was at Les Rochers reading occupied a great deal of her time, at any rate in the autumn and winter. But from September 1675 to March 1676 she only mentions a history of France, a life of Becket, and Nicole, whom she was reading the whole winter. During the summer and autumn (June to October) of 1680, though she says, "Nous lisons beaucoup", she only mentions Nicole and Descartes, while for the long sojourn from September 1684 to August 1685 she does not refer to a single book. On the other hand during her first visit after the separation from Mme de Grignan

—June to December 1671—and her last and longest visit—June 1689 to October 1690—she mentions a fair number of works, especially during the last visit. It is instructive to contrast her tastes during these two periods. For the earlier one we find Petrarch and Tasso, *Cléopatre*, the life of Bertrand Du Guesclin, French history, the letters of Saint-Cyran and the inevitable Nicole. For the later one we have Hamon's *La Prière perpétuelle*, Vertot's *Conjuration*, Fléchier's *Vie de Théodose*, Pascal, Nicole, and long and serious works of Church history and theological controversy—Bossuet's *Variations*, Maimbourg's *Histoire de l'Arianisme*, a *Histoire de l'Eglise*, Arnauld's *De la Perpétuité de la Foi* and Abbadie's *De la Vérité de la Foi chrétienne*. Moreover, Mme de Sévigné's references to the works that she had read in her younger days are much fewer than in 1670. This shews that during the middle years of her life her interest in literature turned from poetry and romance and drama to grave and solid works, historical or otherwise, especially to those which dealt either with Church history or religious controversy. She also read more books of devotion.

Remembering then the necessarily incomplete record of her reading that her letters give us, let us consider for a moment Mme de Sévigné's taste in literature. It was evidently that of a highly intelligent woman, of one who was in touch with the literary world, but who had decided opinions of her own, of one who did not pretend to be a literary critic, but who frankly praised and criticised what she read, of one, in short, who read to please herself and not in order to appear learned, or well-informed, or up to date. The record of her reading is therefore chiefly interesting for the light that it throws on her own character.

To begin with, we may note what perhaps should be called her conservatism, but what I prefer to call her loyalty. For she was loyal to her books in the same way that she was loyal to her friends. This is especially true with regard to Corneille, to whom she clung all the more closely when his powers were declining and Racine was taking his place in public opinion. And this loyalty, or, if you like, this conservatism, meant independence of judgment. She continued to read Montaigne long after he had gone out of favour, and she could enjoy the *coups d'épée* of La Calprenède when not only his romances but also those of Mlle de Scudéry had gone out of fashion. But she welcomed the writers of the reign of Louis XIV with an instinct for great literature which never failed her. Pascal, Molière, and La Fontaine irresistibly appealed to her. In them she found wit, humour, imagination, knowledge of human nature, and in La Fontaine that descriptive power which she herself had in so remarkable a degree. She does not often criticise from the point of view of style, but she knows at once whether a work is well or ill written and she does not hesitate to say so. I doubt whether the higher qualities of poetry appealed to her, but it is difficult to be positive about this, because poetry meant nothing to her daughter.

We have seen that she read history with marked enjoyment. It appealed alike to her imagination and her interest in human nature. She read it not so much for instruction either in political or social matters, as for incident and character. She was thrilled by Josephus's account of the siege of Jotopata, and she followed with sympathy the fortunes of Germanicus. She liked biographies and took a pleasure in the "portraits" which were a feature of the age. Those in Bourdaloue's sermons especially pleased her, though, as we have seen, she was perhaps wrong in supposing that they were portraits of her friends and acquaintances. But it was the moral element in his sermons, the boldness with which he attacked the fashionable vices of the day, that made him her favourite preacher. It was the same interest in morals that drew her to Nicole and kept her a constant admirer, forgiving his dullness and monotony for the sake of his solid reasoning and sound ethical teaching.

A reader herself, she rejoiced to find her granddaughter Pauline a "dévoreuse de livres" as she calls her in a letter of 15 January 1689, when she was fifteen. "J'aime mieux qu'elle en avale de mauvais que si elle n'aimait point à lire." Then she goes on to make suggestions for her reading: "Has she read Lucian? Can she appreciate the Little Letters? She must read history: if she does not find it to her account, I pity her. As for good devotional books, if she does not like them, so much the worse for her." As for works treating of morals, she would not have her put her little nose into Montaigne or Charron; she is too young for writers of that kind. The true moral teaching for young people of that age is to be had from good conversation, from fables or from history. And in a letter written a week earlier she recommends Tasso's *Aminta*, Guarini's *Il Pastor fido*, but not Ariosto—"il y a des endroits fâcheux". She had better keep to poetry. Guicciardini is too long; Davila is good, but Mme de Sévigné does not like Italian prose. In French she must read history, and let her begin with Fléchier's *Life of Theodosius*.

It is interesting to compare this advice with Fénelon's classical treatise, *De l'Education des Filles*, published in 1687, but written about 1680. Like Mme de Sévigné he recommends the reading of Greek, Roman and French history and that of other modern countries. But, contrary to the general idea, he thinks the study of Spanish and Italian harmful, for it may lead to the reading of dangerous books. Pauline, however, was under her mother's eye and she would not have been allowed to read a "dangerous book" like Ariosto. Indeed, Fénelon only approved profane works in general provided they were not dangerous for the passions. He would certainly not have approved of either the *Aminta* or the *Pastor fido*, in both of which the main subject is love. But it must be remembered that his object was a practical one, how to fit a girl for her vocation, whether it was marriage or a convent. It was therefore natural that on the intellectual side he should be less liberal than Mme de Sévigné. Moreover, though he wrote his treatise at the instance of the Duchesse de Beauvilliers and primarily for the benefit of her daughters, he meant it more or less for girls in general, not for a particular girl whose education was being carefully supervised by her mother and her grandmother.

Mme de Maintenon's views on the reading of girls were even less liberal than Fénelon's. Under the influence of the reaction from the performances of *Esther* and *Athalie* she condemned all profane literature. She regarded all novels as bad, "because they dealt only with vices and passions", and Roman history as dangerous, "because it puffed up the mind". She would have the mistresses at Saint-Cyr give their pupils mere notions of history. Her object was even more severely practical than Fénelon's, and the girls at Saint-Cyr, though of noble birth, belonged to a poorer class than those for whom Fénelon wrote. In a discourse which Fénelon gave at Saint-Cyr in 1691 on the religious life he declaimed against "cette vaine curiosité des livres", and he added "O quel amusement pernicieux dans ce qu'on appelle lectures les plus solides."

CHRONOLOGICAL NOTE

1626 (5 February). Birth.

1644 Marriage to the Marquis de Sévigné.

1646 Birth of Marguerite.

1648 Birth of Charles.

1651 Death of M. de Sévigné.

1663 Marguerite de Sévigné presented at Court.

1669 (29 January). Marriage of Marguerite to the Comte de Grignan.

1670 Birth of Marie-Blanche de Grignan.

1671 (4 February). Mme de Grignan leaves Paris.
Birth of Louis-Provence de Grignan.
May to December. Mme de Sévigné at Les Rochers.

1673 July to October. Mme de Sévigné at Grignan.

1674 February to May 1675. Mme de Grignan in Paris.

1675 September to March 1676. Mme de Sévigné at Les Rochers.

1676 May and June. Mme de Sévigné at Vichy.
December to June 1677. Mme de Grignan in Paris.

1677 Mme de Sévigné goes to live at the Hôtel de Carnavalet.
September. Mme de Sévigné at Vichy.
October to September 1679. Mme de Grignan at Paris.

1680 May to October. Mme de Sévigné at Les Rochers.
November to September 1688. Mme de Grignan in Paris.

1684 Marriage of Charles de Sévigné.
September to August 1685. Mme de Sévigné at Les Rochers.

1687 September. Mme de Sévigné at Bourbon-les-Bains.

1689 June to October 1690. Mme de Sévigné at Les Rochers.

1690 October to December 1691. Mme de Sévigné at Grignan.

1694 May to April 1696. Mme de Sévigné at Grignan.

1695 Marriage of Pauline de Grignan to M. de Simiane. Marriage of Louis-Provence de Grignan.

1696 (17 April). Death of Mme de Sévigné.

It will be seen that Mme de Grignan spent about fourteen and a half years of her married life up to her mother's death in Paris. During this time she was separated from her from September 1684 to August 1685, and in September 1687, when her mother was at Bourbon.

INDEX

INDEX

INDEX

INDEX

Princesse de Clèves, La, 81
Provinciales, Lettres, 80, 96, 118, 119, 151

Quevedo, 142
Quinault, Philippe, 17, 123
Quintilian, 143

Rabelais, 94, 113
Racan, 115
Racine, 50, 120–2, 133, 147, 150, 153
Rapin, René, 49, 50, 144, 145
Reims, Archbishop of (Charles Maurice Le Tellier), 72
Renaudot, Théophraste, 7
Rennes, Bishop of, 81
Retz, Cardinal de, 30, 53–6, 73, 120
Richelieu, Duc de, 12
    Duchesse de, 12
Rue Courteau-Vilain, 65
    Culture-Sainte-Catherine, 65
    Thorigny, 65

Sablé, Mme de, 113
Saint-Amant, 87, 115
Saint-Aubin, Seigneur de (Charles de Coulanges), 63–4
Saint-Cyr, 152
Saint-Cyran, Abbé de, 97, 149
Saint-Dié, 85
Saint-Germain, Mme de, 71
Saint-Hilaire, Armand de, 9
Saint-Simon, *passim*
Sanzei, Mme de, 72
Sarasin, Jean-François, 115
Saumur, 84, 85
Schomberg, Mme de, 12, 69
    Maréchal de, 12, 69, 140
Scott, Sir Walter, 139
Scudéry, Mlle de, 116, 117, 118, 150
Segrais, Jean Regnaud de, 115
Sévigné, Charles de (husband of Mme de Sévigné), 53, 136
    Charles de (son of Mme de Sévigné), 83, 89, 91, 92, 93, 94

Mme de (wife of Charles de), 90, 91, 93
    Renaud de, 95, 96
Sforza, Duchesse de, 16 *n.* 1
Simiane, Mme de. *See* Grignan, Pauline de
Soanen, Père, 100
Soubise, Mme de, 16, 21

Tacitus, 138
Tarente, Princesse de, 85
Tasso, 61, 142, 149, 152
Têtu, Abbé, 12, 13, 34, 60, 70, 74
Théophile. *See* Viau
Thianges, Mme de, 4, 15, 16 *n.* 1, 70
Torcy, Marquis de, 48
Toulouse, Comte de, 44
Tours, 84, 85
Tréville, M. de, 20, 98
Troyes, Bishop of, 71
Turenne, 9, 67, 85, 104, 130, 131

Vardes, Marquis de, 52
Vatel, 7
Vauban, 22
Veret, 84
Verneuil, Duc de, 46
    Duchesse de, 46, 73, 74, 75
Versailles, *passim*
Vertot, Abbé de, 140, 149
Viau, Théophile de, 115
Vichy, 15, 71, 80, 90
Villars, M. de, 23
Vins, Marquis de, 40
    Mme de (Mlle Ladvocat), 39–40, 73, 74, 75
Virgil, 143
Voiture, 60, 115
Voltaire, 5, 111, 135, 137

Walpole, Horace, 3, 78–9, 111
Wharton, Tom, 3
William of Orange, 10

For EU product safety concerns, contact us at Calle de José Abascal, 56–1°, 28003 Madrid, Spain or eugpsr@cambridge.org.

www.ingramcontent.com/pod-product-compliance
Ingram Content Group UK Ltd.
Pitfield, Milton Keynes, MK11 3LW, UK
UKHW012341130625
459647UK00009B/451